CHARISMATIC
SOCIAL ACTION

CHARISMATIC SOCIAL ACTION

Reflection/Resource Manual

by

Sheila Macmanus Fahey

PAULIST PRESS
New York, N.Y./Ramsey, N.J.

Library of Congress
Catalog Card Number: 77-70633

ISBN: 0-8091-2014-3

Published by Paulist Press
Editorial Office: 1865 Broadway, New York, N.Y. 10023
Business Office: 545 Island Road, Ramsey, N.J. 07446

Printed and bound in the
United States of America

Contents

Get out there yourselves an' stop feedin' offa me. . . . I've done enough world shakin' for awhile; you do the rest of it and send me a postcard.

Cool Hand Luke

To Jimmy Clifford

Foreword

Sheila Macmanus Fahey has done a great service in providing this book as an aid to those who wish to engage in social ministry, even though it may not please those who are looking for simple or magic answers.

The social responsibility of the first Christian community (first parish? first prayer group?) is described in Acts 2:42-47 and 4:32-35, where it says that they "lived together and owned everything in common" and "none of their members was ever in want." This social consciousness was translated in many different ways down through the centuries of Church history.

The modern social teaching of the Church, responding to problems created by the industrial and technological revolution, dates from Pope Leo XIII in 1891 to the present, roughly eighty-five years. This teaching is a great gift and treasure which the Catholic community should be proud to possess and share with others. Just as the historic churches are indebted to the Pentecostals for calling our attention to the central role of the Holy Spirit in our lives, so we Catholics should be proud to share with other denominations our tradition of social teaching.

The capstone of this prophetic teaching is *Justice in the World,* issued by the World Synod of Catholic Bishops meeting in Rome in 1971, which states: "Action on behalf of justice and participation in the transformation of the world fully appear to us as a *constitutive* dimension of the preaching of the Gospel, or, in other words, of the Church's mission for the redemption of the human race and its liberation from every oppressive situation."

Justice in the World teaches that working for justice and the transformation of society is not just for a few, but for everyone; not peripheral to Christian life, but central, essential; not optional, but necessary, mandatory; not just a matter of charity, but of justice. In other words, if our parishes and prayer groups

are not proclaiming justice and working for justice, we are
neither proclaiming nor living the *full* Gospel; something is
essentially wrong with our Christian life.

The social teaching of the Church tells us to be concerned
not about principles alone, but also about translating our values
and principles into political action. It tells us that we cannot be
concerned only about our own nation, but must see the entire
human community as one family of our one Father. We are
called not to flee the world, but rather to transform it. We form
Christian community, not for isolation, but for power (cf.
Ephesians 4). We are called to change not only hearts, but also
social structures and institutions. It is not a choice of either/or,
but both/and.

The psalms tell us that God hears the cries of the oppressed,
of orphans and widows. We who claim to be God's people can
do no less. Heaven forbid that we might be the ones causing them
to cry out. The Scriptures are filled with statements that our
God is a God of justice, mercy, and compassion. We who claim
to be God's people must be a people of justice, mercy, and
compassion.

The Church and the world would be richly blessed if the
very best from charismatic renewal and from social action
could be fused. On December 18, 1975, twenty-six persons from
North and South America met near Phoenix, Arizona to try
to move in that direction. Their statement, while only a beginning, might be helpful to those who will use this book.

Charismatic Renewal and Social Action

First of all, we would like to declare that the movements
for Social Justice and the Charismatic Renewal are two
necessary dimensions of the work of the Spirit in our time.
We believe that the fullness of God's work will be achieved
through their fruitful interaction. We strongly affirm this
because in our own lives and ministries we are experi-
encing an extraordinary vitality flowing from such interaction.

We view the social, cultural, and political aspects of the world as reflections of the incarnation and in need of being transformed, not as something to be ignored or shunned. We affirm that an essential part of Christian life is to work in the world not only to renew persons but to renew society and its structures. We must be concerned about social structures because (1) they must reflect the justice and love of God and (2) unjust structures wound and even destroy individuals, families and the quality of human life in all its aspects. These are urgent times. Christians must take appropriate action against social evil, or a prophetic stance against an authority which would condone them.

But we cannot create a fully human society until we become new men and women in Christ. Without a radical conversion to Christ, we are simply building on sand, since a just society can only be produced by just people. The Spirit of Jesus can destroy barriers of suspicion and hatred and build bridges of understanding, trust and love.

The same power of the Spirit experienced in the charismatic renewal to change individual lives and to built community is also bringing a new power and effectiveness to the movement for social justice. To date, the movements by and large have worked separately; but the full Gospel requires their powerful interaction.

Furthermore, it is in actually performing the works of justice that we ourselves grow into mature men and women of justice.

The social doctrine of the Catholic Church is a prophetic message for our times: "Action on behalf of justice and participation in the transformation of the world fully appear to us as a constitutive dimension of the preaching of the Gospel" (World Synod of Catholic Bishops, Rome 1971).

Rev. Marvin A. Mottet

Introduction

When Jim and I began with a small prayer group in New Orleans in 1969, we immediately began to wonder if it would be possible someday for charismatics to connect their upper room prayer experience to the outer world in an organized effort at "social action."

Throughout the following years whenever we would meet our friend Harold Cohen, he would assure us that the movement was still in its infancy and that he and many others were envisioning the next stage of growth to include an element of organized Christian service.

A few months ago I was gratified to read that a Catholic Charismatic Renewal Movement leader, Kevin Ranaghan, had said that the movement was now growing from its apologetic stage toward its prophetic stage.[1]

This book is to be a resource book, then, for prophets— both in and out of the charismatic movement—who, without fear and with unremitting effort, commit themselves to calling the world back to the humane vision of Jesus Christ.

The first chapter of this book is an orientation to service.

Chapters 2-10 are structurally parallel as they acquaint the reader with aspects of, and approaches to, healing some of the more prominent wounds of our society and world. Chapters 2-10 are structured, as you will note, in an Observe/Judge/Act framework. They each include: (1) an informational introduction to the issue, (2) a brief study bibliography, (3) comments on the issue in light of the Christian message, (4) questions for individual/group reflection/discussion, and (5) fifteen to thirty suggested actions. I emphasize that the actions are *suggested*. The resulting ideas your group comes up with after studying the materials may be entirely different from my own suggestions. I would hope that they would be different in that they would be molded to the needs of your own city or community.

Chapter 11 has five issues which were either too massive to

treat or had been touched on in foregoing chapters. Each issue has a very brief introduction and a social inquiry or two to get your group started. Special thanks go to Rev. Marvin A. Mottet and the Social Action Department of the Diocese of Davenport. Five of the social inquiries—Catholic Schools, Public Schools, Political Action, Peace, and Housing—were adapted with permission from *Social Inquiries for Parish Christian Service Committees* published by the Department.

At the end of the book you will find an alphabetized action address list containing every address noted in the book as well as some additional ones I thought you might need for your work. Space is left for you to add your local action addresses.

Some of the service suggestions in the book are the result of a random query of fifty charismatic groups across the country. Among those I wish to thank for responding are: Rev. Francis A. Messing of Citronelle, Alabama; Sr. Roberta Tenbrink, R.S.M., and Gary Wright, S.J., of New Jerusalem community in Cincinnati; Rev. Ronald J. Reichs of Maranatha Community in Sioux City; Patrick Bruen of Community of God's Mercy in Dearborn, Michigan; John H. Steubeck of Lemon Grove, California; Fr. H. of Benet Lake, Wisconsin; Sr. Mary of Kimberly, Wisconsin; Robert De Rouen, S.J., of Holy Spirit Renewal in Denver; Lawrence Elizardi of the Jesuit Fathers of Albuquerque; Fr. Thomas L. Bill, C.S.C., at the University of Portland Prayer Group; William J. Rademacher of the Shepherd's Prayer Community in St. Cloud, Minnesota. Thanks also to those nameless who responded.

Some background material and bibliographical materials in certain areas of concern were kindly shared with me by professionals in the marketplace. They include Joe Putnam for Race Relations, John Boyle for Drugs and Addiction, Tom Laughlin and Dottie Lastrapes for the Aged, Dave Boileau and the staff of the Institute of Social Order of Loyola University of New Orleans for Correctional Reform, Consumerism, and Hunger.

Thank you to Harold Cohen, S.J., for getting himself to Notre Dame in April of 1969, to Robert Heyer of Paulist Press for editing, to Jane Smart Chenevert and Rita Barrett Macmanus for encouraging. Most especially I want to express my heartfelt thanks to my marriage partner, Jim, for his inspiration, occasional proofreading assistance in the preparation of Part Two of Chapter 1, and authorship of the chapter on Media. Thanks to Matt, N.J., and Adam for loving me.

Use the book rather than let it use you. No prayer group or parish will be able to tackle all the issues as a whole. I suggest you divide and conquer.

Any light that is shed herein and any good that derives from this book have as their source that Light which is the Holy Spirit. Any darkness please blame on me. Let nothing be left undone. Let no one be left unchallenged! Praise the Lord!

1
ORIENTATION
TO
SERVICE

Part One

Contrary to what we heard from the social action movements of the 60's, there is no "social gospel" per se at the base of the Church's service activities in the world. When the Church acts in building the earth and healing the wounds of the "secular" city, it acts *in consequence* of the good news which Jesus was/preached.

We cannot separate the person of Jesus from his work. So if we put our faith in Jesus Christ we consequently become work, become sacrifice in his name. We see, then, the blood kinship of faith and love. Joseph Ratzinger says, ". . . to confess one's faith in Christ . . . means to recognize the man who needs me as the Christ in the form in which he comes to meet me here and now; it means understanding the challenge of love as the challenge of faith. . . . The 'I' (which is Jesus and which is you and I as Christians) . . . is completely derived from the 'Thou' of the Father and lived for the 'You' of men."[2] God called Jesus; Jesus responded to God. We are the beneficiaries of his obedience.

Jesus was in God's service as his submission to baptism testifies. "And a voice came from heaven, 'You are my Son, the Beloved; my favor rests on you' " (Mk. 1:9-11). With these words the Old Testament prophecy of the "servant of Yahweh" (Is. 42:1) is fulfilled. Jesus' life will be totally lived for others.

Through his perfect model of Servant, Jesus exhorts us to be God's servants among men. We have submitted to baptism and we have received the Holy Spirit. The value of our baptism is seen when we live out the ethical implications of its challenge. The gift of our baptism is God's, but it takes an act of our will to fulfill it. It is not enough to pray quietly in one's room or less quietly in a larger group. These attitudes and stages of prayer are vital but our lights must also shine in our individual-to-individual, individual-to-group, and group-to-group relationships. Our lights must shine to non-charismatic renewal movement persons—within our own homes, within our parishes, through-out our larger local communities, our nation, and the world.

In a passage of Matthew's gospel which enlarges upon the theme of light, Jesus teaches: "You are the light of the world. A city built on a hill-top cannot be hidden. No one lights a lamp to put it under a tub; they put it on the lamp-stand where it shines for everyone in the house. In the same way your light must shine in the sight of men, so that seeing your good works they may give praise to your Father in heaven" (Mt. 5:14-16). The "you" which Jesus uses in this passage is a collective "you." Be individuals for others, yes, but also be a community of believers, a Church for others.

The purpose of community is to bring forward the presence of Jesus Christ for consideration by the entire human race. Our worship is secondary to and in service of this mission. Our com-munity, whether prayer group or parish, is to serve the King-dom, not vice versa. So a *primary* reason for having a commu-nity of believers in Jesus Christ is not to pray together but to introduce the world into his presence. (Of course one of the ways to do this is through prayer.)

Our reasons to be have to do with message, community, and service: the Word which the Church proclaims (*didache*), our fellowship in the life of the Holy Spirit (*koinonia*), and our service to the Christian community and to the entire human family (*diakonia*).

There has been controversy over the years as to whether the Church should be the herald of the apocalypse or the proph-et calling the world back to its holy project. The Church, in preaching the Kingdom of God as Jesus, does not have to be *ei-ther* apocalyptic *or* prophetic, but can be comfortable with being *both* apocalyptic *and* prophetic. We need not have our eyes so totally on the coming personal reign of Jesus (as St. Paul also occasionally and understandably did) that we neglect our role as prophets within the Church and within our society.

As Vatican II says, "(The Church) teaches that a hope related to the end of time does not diminish the importance of intervening duties, but rather undergirds the acquittal of them with fresh incentives."[3] We see in the Jesus event more a life *through* death than a life *after* death. So, if aspects of the Church or society are not aligned with the breathtaking message which is Jesus, we, like Amos and Hosea before us, must "take to the hustings."

As powerful and important as personal conversions are, it is not enough for us to be satisfied with individuals saying with meaning, "Jesus is my Lord!" A concomitant goal should be that that elusive "person" which is the society should take on the face of Jesus—in its institutions, in its technology, in its social mores. What we are dealing with here is the category of sin referred to as "social sin." The *Sourcebook on Poverty, Development and Justice* devotes an entire section (III) to "The Concept of Social Sin." In discussing the Synod document "Justice in the World" the sourcebook says:

> A major theme in Biblical theology is, of course, the theme of sin and redemption. It is this theme which the Synod document on world justice explicitly picks up and develops in a social context, thereby explicating a new dimension in Church social teaching—the dimensions of "social sin." While this category of social sin can be found in earlier teachings, it is not found with the explicitness and detail with which the Synod debated the topic and wrote of it in its final document.
>
> In general, social sin refers to:
>
> (1) Structures that oppress human beings, violate human dignity, stifle freedom, impose gross inequality.
>
> (2) Situations that promote and facilitate individual acts of selfishness.
>
> (3) The complicity of persons who do not take responsibility for the evil being done.[4]

In the Bible both sin and grace are addressed *both* to the individual *and* to the community—everything has both a personal and a social meaning. The incarnation holds a message for the *entire* community.

As Colin Williams has said so beautifully, "God does not want only individuals to be saved. He wants his whole creative work saved. . . . Therefore he wants us to involve ourselves in serving his creation. . . . We cannot just look to the saving of our souls."[5] This involving process and the final coming to wholeness are gifts of God. Our acting in this process is our response in obedience to God's grace.

Before we can begin the work of sacrificial witness to "secular" man in the United States of America, *we must get his attention.* I am reminded of the stories brought home by the missionaries in years past—"The people are not able to listen to the Word because they are distracted by their empty stomachs." The conclusion was that the most immediate way to witness to what Jesus is about was to help the people to feed themselves.

Modern man is distracted by many things. In order to get his attention (for if the Church does not speak to contemporary man, it is speaking to an empty auditorium) we as Christians must truly be in the world but not of the world. We must inform ourselves in order to recognize the wounds, distractions, and the forces of evil in our world. In this way we will train ourselves to speak a language which contemporary man understands. The content of the kerygma will remain the same but the language we use (if we choose to educate ourselves to the language and models to which contemporary man responds) must be in some cases different and in other cases merely more precise and on a surer course to the heart of individual and societal ruptures.

We could adopt the Jesuit motto, "Ad Majorem Dei Gloriam," to the greater glory of God. But what is the glory of God? Jesus' glory was his victory over death/darkness/evil/estrangement. His glory was the reconciliation of God and man in the paschal sacrifice.

"The basic moral demands of Jesus are repentance, faith, and discipleship. What is most important is the total personal option for God's will, so that God's will may unfold before the believer step by step for the rest of his life."[6] If being Jesus' disciples is at the heart of morality, we must be, like Jesus, reconcilers. We must be, like Jesus, healers.

In his book *Pentecostalism: A Theological Viewpoint*, Donald Gelpi points out that the normative charismatic experience is the experience of the person Jesus. Truly Jesus *is* the message we are called upon to mediate to others. In order to do this we must attend to our relationship with God in the Holy Spirit while offering the possibility of this relationship to every person.

Jesus gave us a seven point program in Matthew 25:36-41: (1) feed the hungry; (2) give drink to the thirsty; (3) shelter the homeless; (4) clothe the naked; (5) visit the sick; (6) visit the imprisoned; (7) bury the dead. Large segments of our society are disenfranchised. Our efforts to be agents of Christ's healing power must be as large as these needs.

How do the "why's" of service and the rich prayer life coincide? For the charismatic, prayer is the central means of recognizing the will of the Father. Morton Kelsey sees prayer as a threefold process. First, the person is shaped in a religious environment (at the Eucharist, meeting with the prayer group, in Christian education situations, etc.). He touches liturgy and the historical wealth of his Christian faith. In the second stage of prayer the person turns inward and listens to the Holy Spirit in order to find the particularization of the message in himself. Here he finds the answer to the question, "What is your will in the particular situation of my own life and mission?"

In the third stage (which makes the prayer process whole), the person turns outward to express what he has found to others. It is possible to have both the first and second stages of prayer (that is, one can participate in the liturgy of the Church, pray in community at every opportunity, and share a rich communion with God in his private prayer life), but if one does not reach out to one's brothers one is not fully in unison with the Sacrifice (Jesus Christ).

Prayer, in order to be whole, must lead to loving human action at some level, action going from God through me to another or other human being(s), structures, situations. Activity is a dominant feature of Christian prayer. Prayer must have rational value in loving others. Unless a Christian movement has some aspects of loving service it cannot be legitimately called Christian.

It is for the members of the Catholic Charismatic Renewal Movement and other charismatics with the force of the Holy Spirit whom we espouse, to join with Christians and right-minded others in sending the world a Message. The Church (in all its members) must be an agent of healing. As the saying on the banner goes, "It is not faith *or* works; it is not faith *and* works; it is faith *that* works."

Part Two

Fr. Louis Putz suggested in 1958 that the Christian must work on creating an awareness of social responsibility within himself. You might well ask, "Where do I and my group start?"

Putz suggested four steps: (1) know the mind of the Church; (2) get acquainted with social problems; (3) get involved with social problems; (4) dedicate your life to social improvement.[7]

The best indicator of the "mind of the Church" (with which I am acquainted) in regard to social responsibility is the *Pastoral Constitution on the Church in the Modern World* of the documents of the Second Vatican Council. In addition the *Decree on the Apostolate of the Laity* has much to say about the norms for all Christian apostles.[8] John Deedy has said, "The urgency of an expanded and sharpened Christological presence in the world is why so many placed such large hopes in Vatican Council II and its schema on the Church in the Modern World. That schema emerged from the Council as a pastoral constitution dealing with the very sorts of activities that the committed are today caught up in. If it is incongruous, therefore, to speak of the witness of the intellectual, the social activist and others as being inspirational and as contributing to one's spiritual life, then we may as well rub the Constitution on the Church in the Modern World off the history books of religion and out of the Catholic experience."[9]

The bibliographical and introductory material included in

each problem area presented in this book should acquaint you and your group with specific social problems. Another very important source of information about social problems is the secular press. Try to get in the habit of critically reading the newspapers each day and reading at least one good weekly news magazine. In this way, you will be doing your daily "homework" in social action and involvement. The changing profiles of the issues in this book can be seen in the daily press.

Getting involved with social problems will come naturally for your group as you continue to inform yourselves and to touch the lives and needs of more people. This is happening now all over the country. One small segment of a Catholic Charismatic Renewal Movement group gets involved with a specific social need, for example, concern for the aged. Before you know it, many of the larger group are supporting their efforts with needed prayers and all manner of tangible assistance.

The ways in which you and your group choose to get involved with any of the major social problems of today will depend on what you have observed about the problem situation and what judgments you have come to regarding what you can do to contribute to its healing. More will be said about this when we speak of specific methodology.

As for Father Putz's fourth point—dedicate your life to social improvement—it is an infinitesimal step from dedicating your life to Christ to dedicating your life to his creation. It is most important that you have life to dedicate. You must care for your body as well as you care for your spiritual needs. I recall praying occasionally in groups where some of the participants were up until 3 A.M. three nights a week in group prayer. When doctors suggest that for most people the first three hours of the morning after waking can be the most productive of our day, I often wonder how much energy these persons have to serve the Lord the morning after. Your biology has very much to do with your effectiveness for Christ. The time inventory at the end of this chapter will assist you in reorganizing your energies.

Now what about problem solving methodology? To aid in our understanding of the dynamics of problem solving, let us turn to John Dewey's psychological bases for problem solving:

(1) Recognize a specific lack or disorientation.
(2) Examine the nature, scope, and implications.
(3) Look for a new orientation.
(4) Examine several alternative solutions.
(5) Choose the best solution for your particular case. Act upon it.[10]

So we have:

OBSERVE: Recognize a specific lack.
Examine its nature, scope, and implications.

JUDGE: (Scripture references with sound exegesis helpful here)
In the light of Christian principles, what should the ideal situation be? Commit as a group to pray about the matter. Consciously listen for and be open to God's voice in the matter. Look for a new (Christian) orientation.

ACT: Examine alternative solutions.
Choose the best solution(s).
Act upon it (them).

It is best in your approach to a problem to deal in specifics or particulars as Dewey suggests. In this process it is important to note a clear distinction between a general problem and a specific problem.

General Problem: Many people are addicted to drugs.

Specific Problem: Most of the basketball players at Eastside High School are on uppers and downers.

or

Television advertising encourages drug taking.

or

I am an alcohol abuser.

or

Drunk drivers caused more deaths on our highways last year than the number of Americans killed in the entire Vietnam war.

Here now are some practical guidelines in getting Christ's message out whether as an individual or as a member of your prayer community. *Organize your thoughts so that you can tell someone else about them.*

In regard to speaking out:

(1) Include an introduction, body, and conclusion.
(2) Tell your audience (be it the mayor or the women's guild or the P.T.A. or your pastor) what you are going to tell them; tell them; tell them what you told them (otherwise known as the three T's of good speech communication— R. E. Harlan).
(3) Motivate people to action by pointing out how the problem directly affects them, and motivate them by pointing out how they can be part of the solution.
(4) Make sure the action you decide upon
    (a) is specific and speaks directly to the problem;
    (b) is within the realm of possibility for you or the group.

In regard to "writing out":

(1) When? Often. Whenever your group has decided to take action in this way on a specific problem. Whenever you feel your individual vote should be registered—whether with a television programmer, your congressperson, the local movie theater manager, the welfare department, the school board, the mayor, etc.
(2) How? With pen or typewriter and paper. Keep in one safe place pen, paper, and stamps and the action address list. (See appendix for complete list—cut it out, mount it on cardboard if necessary and keep it with your writing materials. Problem area addresses will also be found in the related chapter.) When you write be brief, polite, and to the point.

Where do you find time for this? The following exercise is adapted from Strategy Number 33 of the book *Values Clarification* by Simon, Howe, and Kirschenbaum.[11]

The Pie of Life

This exercise asks us to inventory our lives—to see how we actually *do* spend our time. This information is needed if we hope to move from what we are getting to what we want to get out of life. Let us look at how you use your typical day. Divide this circle into four quarters using dotted lines. Each slice represents six hours. Now estimate how many hours or parts of an hour you spend on each of the following areas on a typical weekday. (You may choose to work up an inventory on Saturday and Sunday after this exercise.) How many hours do you spend:

(1) On SLEEP?
(2) On PRAYER as such (group or private)?
(3) At WORK, at a job that earns you money?
(4) With FRIENDS, socializing, playing sports, etc.?
(5) On CHAUFFERING?
(6) ALONE, playing, reading, watching TV?
(7) On HOUSEWORK and ERRANDS?
(8) With FAMILY, including mealtimes?
(9) On MISCELLANEOUS other pastimes?

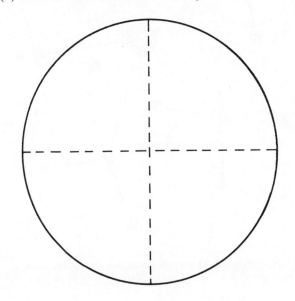

Your estimates will not be exact, but they should add up to 24, the number of hours in everyone's day. Draw slices in your pie to represent proportionately the part of the day you spend on each category. Answer these questions:

(1) Are you satisfied with the relative sizes of your slices?

(2) Ideally, how big would you want each slice to be? Draw your ideal pie.

(3) Realistically, is there anything you can do to begin to change the size of some of your slices?

In your personal and group approaches to organized loving service, keep in mind the ripple effect of your work. Consider the following model:

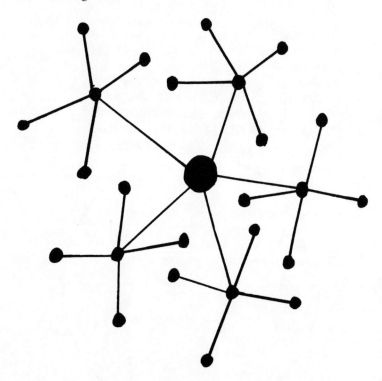

Sociological Model of Human Communication/
Sphere of Influence

As we act as opinion leaders, so those who follow us are in their own turn other opinion leaders. Thus, our sphere of influence spreads from our small group to an ever expanding larger sphere of influence.

A Word on Parish Life

One of the major spheres of influence beyond the family and prayer group for the charismatic is his parish or regular worshiping community. The parish should be one of the prime beneficiaries of the fruits of the charismatic renewal movement.

Many charismatic groups queried indicated they were not involved in formal social action work but were directing much energy to parish life and parish renewal through existing parish structures and organizations. Some examples of this are charismatic renewal movement members serving as CCD teachers, extraordinary ministers of the Eucharist, parish council members, and prayer group organizers. Others are caring for the parish plant facilities, painting the parish school, conducting a book ministry to serve the parish with the good word, or participating in the work of the parish social action ministry.

One group in St. Cloud, Minnesota has found that "the most effective social servants are those who rest secure in solid community relationships." The mutual support and gifts the parish and charismatic share should not be undervalued or minimized.

In conclusion, this book can be used either in or out of parish structures. Those in need are everywhere. As Christians the call to informed, reflective action is clear. The Observe/Judge/Act methodology has been tried and found to be highly effective.

Many sense that something is indeed afoot in the universe. Let it be!

2
THE AGED

There is only one solution if old age is not to be an absurd parody of our former life, and that is to go on pursuing ends that give our existence a meaning—devotion to individuals, to groups or to causes, social, political, intellectual or creative work. In spite of the moralists' opinion to the contrary, in old age we should wish still to have passions strong enough to prevent us turning in upon ourselves. One's life has value so long as one attributes value to the life of others, by means of love, friendship, indignation, compassion.

Simone de Beauvoir

I. Introduction

An anecdote may serve to put the basic problem of the aged in America in immediate perspective. While preparing my files for the writing of this book, a friend looked over the chapter titles and asked, "Couldn't you combine the chapters on the sick and on the aged and save yourself some work?" I replied in the negative.

The myth persists that all older persons are sick or on their way to becoming sick. "Untrue!" say gerontologists, social scientists, and the aged themselves. Although a significant number of the elderly do have disabilities, the large proportion of those over 65 years of age are not seriously impaired physically, nor are they senile.[1] To lay the older-people-are-always-sick myth to rest, reflect for a moment on those persons you know who are age 65 or older.[2]

How many Americans are included in this age group? At present, one in every ten American citizens is at least 65 years of age. One-third of this group is over 75.[3] There are more older people alive today than at any time in history. The present life expectancy at birth in our country is age 70 for males, and age 74 for females.[4]

From 1900 to 1950 the number of Americans 65 and older essentially doubled. In the year 2030, if present population projections are accurate, one out of every six persons in our country will be over 65.[5] These projections are considered conservative as they do not take into account future life lengthening discoveries.

What is aging? Experts tell us that aging involves the death of cells frequently because the cell fails to reproduce itself accurately.[6] But aging is more than just a biological process. Speaking of the aged means speaking of additional topics as diverse and complex as the socio-political processes of aging, the economics of aging,[7] the retirement experience, the institutionalized elderly, and so forth.

One group which has been formed to combat the negative socio-psychological effects of aging is SAGE—Senior Actualization and Growth Exploration. The premise of SAGE's work is "that the 70 year old can grow just as much as the 7 year old, given the same love and encouragement."[8] SAGE works to fight the depression of older people. The exploration is flexible. SAGE centers its attention on inner space using breathing exercises and the supportive mutuality of small groups of older persons.

In some cultures other than our own, the last third of a person's life is looked upon as the special time for spiritual development.

> In . . . countries, such as India, old people get up at 4 or 5 A.M. and go to the ashram for meditation. The early morning is an ideal time to reach the inner self. But in the United States we consider waking early as "insomnia" and we prescribe dangerous and detrimental drugs to keep our old people asleep.[9]

We also try to keep our old people passionless and desire-free. Psychologists tell us that sex at seventy is not only possible but it is good for us. Gerontologists suggest that society must change its inflexible thinking on the subject of sexual activity for older persons because such activity has great mental and physical benefits.[10]

One of the most obvious ways the elderly can be inhibited is by institutionalization. At the beginning of this decade five percent of all old people were residents of long-term institutions. This numbered approximately 610,000 persons, with 108,000 in mental hospitals and the rest in nursing homes and homes for the aged. Nearly all of these long-term residents are supported by public monies.[11] The most ill and cast off persons are in nursing homes, the least ill and more monied persons live in homes for the aged.

My first experience with the institutionalized elderly was ten years ago when I was a nurses' aide in a geriatrics home adjacent to a private hospital. It seemed that the older persons residing there only wanted someone to listen to them. I decided that as soon as my regular work was completed I would spend as much time as possible doing just that. After a couple of days of this arrangement a representative from the other aides came to me. She said that if I continued to spend my free time in the "patients' " rooms instead of (hiding out) in the nurses' station, the other aides would look bad. My response to her will remain between the two of us.

Patients were continually calling out, frequently to people long dead. One patient—catatonic as a result of deep melancholia (over her uselessness, I suspect)—lay motionless except when she erupted in violence and tore the thin skin off her aged forearms.

Disposable bed pads were expensive as was laundry, so patients who wet their beds after 11 P.M. were out of luck until the following day. (I was never on duty after 11 P.M. or the hospital would have had some laundry bill.) As it was a few of the aides did beg, borrow, or steal clean sheets and diapers for their patients.

At that time the monthly cost of living at this home cum hospital (considered far and away one of the better facilities of its kind) was between $400 and $500 per month. I and my coworkers were paid $1.09 per hour.

We must be careful not to think these old people are representative of old people in general. We cannot ignore, on the other hand, the institutionalized elderly whether they are in homes for the aged, mental hospitals, or nursing homes. An expert on the institutionalized elderly says:

> Today many elderly patients who might benefit from home care are being treated in nursing homes. With the availability of federal money to pay for institutional care, nursing homes are attracting some older people who might otherwise be cared for at home.[12]

Suffice it to say—and this applies to all the elderly whether institutionalized or not—that it is very difficult to create "a normal environment for anyone when the essential element of normality—freedom—is removed."[13]

For those elderly who are not in institutions and reach retirement age, the adjustments are of a different sort. Approximately 1.4 million Americans face these adjustments each year.[14]

For the retiree the problem and the answer can frequently be found in the use of leisure time. Retirement means for most older persons two things: substantially more leisure time, and substantially less income. Studies show that increasing numbers of retired persons are making the most of their new-found leisure time. In fact retirement may not deserve the bad name it has been given.

> In one recent national study three out of four of the older persons were satisfied or very satisfied with their lives since retirement.[15]

Many retired and non-retired older persons are spending a fair share of their leisure time in volunteer efforts on behalf of us all.[16] Two such major efforts are the Retired Senior Volunteer Program and the Foster Grandparent Program.[17]

An organization called the "Gray Panthers" is for old people power. The group is a coalition of young and old people working together for social change and social justice. The Panthers believe that the liberation of older people in this country will be a liberation of us all.

The needs of the older people in our society are basically the same needs of any other group: employment, adequate income, transportation, housing, adequate health care, leisure time possibilities, and other services.

How long will we try to keep the old out of sight by ignoring them, firing them, institutionalizing them, or pressuring them to travel around disguised as seventeen-year-olds?

George L. Maddox of the Center for the Study of Aging and Human Development of Duke University says:

> In a society which is now having great difficulty in providing adequate income, housing, social services, and health care for its 20 million older persons, the next few decades should provide a considerable test of

our social ingenuity and our commitment to social justice.[18]

II. Study Bibliography

United States Senate Subcommittee on Aging. *Post-White House Conference on Aging Reports*. U.S. Government Printing Office; Washington, D.C. 20402, 1973.
de Beauvoir, Simone. *The Coming of Age*. G. P. Putnam's Sons: New York, 1972.

The following films on aging are *available for free loan* from the National Audiovisual Center, Distribution Center, Washington, D.C. 20409, 202/763-7420. Specify your preferred play date and two alternatives. You will be permitted to keep the films for three days, and need only pay return postage to the Center.

Title	Description	Length
1. After Autumn	A day in the life of an 82-year-old farmer living alone	10 minutes
2. Step Aside— Step down	A discussion of the problems of aging	20 minutes
3. Seasons	A film dealing with health and rehabilitation	16 minutes

(These films can also be purchased.)

III. Reflections as a Christian

When Jesus asks us to honor our father and our mother (Mt. 19:19; Mk. 10:20) he is not confining us to our own parents. To honor those who have walked the road before we have means to actively love them and respect them as persons. We cannot honor someone with mere words, just as we cannot honor God without loving actions. Our whole posture of living and our total activity must reflect this honor we profess. If we honor those who have lived long whether they are our parents or not, we will show active concern for their continued life, health, and independence.

When Jesus asks us to visit the imprisoned (Mt. 25:37) he may also be including those imprisoned by the conditions which frequently accompany old age. The psychological effects that the older person experiences with the possible loss of work role, diminished income, possible loss of health, changes in the role he or she occupies within the extended family—any or all of these experiences can be at most shattering and at least immobilizing.

When we minister to the needs of older people, and reinforce them in their place in our communities, we are freeing them to be all they can be, and that is what our Christianity is all about.

We must make certain that the older persons in our church, neighborhood, city, and country have the freedom to pursue happiness, the freedom to pursue worthwhile work, the freedom to pursue enjoyable and creative leisure activities. Any treatment that involves less for the elderly is less than human treatment.

A change is necessary in our outlook in this country if we are to be true to these noble goals for human beings. It seems we too often fall prey to stereotyping. The old as pictured on television and in print are frequently either senile or unnecessary appendages who can only advise us on what toilet paper or floor wax to use. Stereotyping is simply not part of a Christian's outlook on life and the living. Jesus made only one demand of all of us: "Come, follow me." If we live his word as he unfolds it for us in our lives, that is our justification regardless of our age.

All human beings have—from the cradle to the grave—their own life project, their godly *raison d'être*. It is not for us (either because someone reaches age 65 or because we have fallen prey to the old age stereotype) to put a limit on what a human being can strive for or accomplish.

In the epistle to the Galatians St. Paul says: "There are no more distinctions between Jew and Greek, slave and free, male and female, but all of you are one in Jesus Christ."

St. Paul could have included "young and old" in his list. Jesus' life and his incredible openness to others, regardless of their sex, social station, age, nationality, or religion, testifies to this.

If we are Christians, then we love and actively want true freedom for all people. Let us see our older brothers and sisters as no less our brothers and sisters than the living Christ they embody. He walks among us with many faces, in many nations, holding many different jobs. He walks as a child and then as an old woman. He is seen sometimes arthritic with a cane, or waiting with legs swollen on a food stamps line. He lives alone and worries about dying alone. He waits for someone to listen to his memories. But mostly he just waits.

Scripture Passages for Reflection

Exodus 20:12
Matthew 19:19
Wisdom 4:7-10
Acts 6:1-6
Proverbs 30:17, 19:26
Psalm 71

IV. Questions for Reflection/Discussion

(1) Read Mark, chapter 3, verses 28 and 29. In what ways do we and does our society sin against the Holy Spirit in our attitude toward and treatment of the aged?

(2) It is very difficult to live a "normal" life in our society when the element of freedom is removed. What are some of the freedoms we deny older persons?

(3) "Mandatory retirement in most jobs at the age of 65 is a necessary evil in our society." Agree or disagree? Why or why not?

(4) Read the quote from Simone de Beauvoir which appears before the introduction to this chapter. What does the way you are living now tell you about the kind of old age you will have?

(5) Describe how you would like to live your older (post age 65) years.

(6) How can you and your group enable those who are old now to live as you describe?

V. Suggested Actions

(1) Visit a nursing home patient on a regular basis.

(2) Offer your meeting place or group hall as a site for daily meals for the elderly.

(3) Start a daily phone service so that each older person in your area who lives alone will receive a daily call.

(4) Transport the elderly on a regular basis to grocery shop, buy their food stamps, meet medical and other appointments. Your group could arrange a regular car pool to do this.

(5) Organize seminars in your area to help older persons fill out Medicare, Medicaid, income tax, property tax, and other forms.

(6) Establish a Retired Senior Volunteer Program and/or a Foster Grandparent Program.[1]

(7) Find out if your city government, parish, or prayer group would be interested in hiring retired tradespersons to do work on homes of those over 65.[2]

(8) On election days offer transportation to the polls.

(9) Start a gift shop which is supplied and staffed by the elderly.

(10) Establish a newsletter for the elderly in your neighborhood, apprising them regularly of events, volunteer opportunities, employment opportunities, etc.

(11) Arrange discounts for the elderly with chain stores and other concerns in your area (drug stores, supermarkets, beauty salons, stores which rent sickroom equipment, restaurants, bus lines, etc.).

(12) Start a day care service for the infirm elderly to enable them to remain at home and not be institutionalized. (Start out by asking your physician, hospital, or social service agency what home care programs are available in your community. Many are covered by Medicare, Medicaid, Blue Cross and other insurance carriers, local welfare agencies.)

(13) Organize a grocery store on wheels (essential items in the back of a truck or van) which goes to the neighborhoods of your elderly on a regular basis.

(14) Offer mini-courses on a variety of subjects for the elderly in your parish or community.

(15) Write the National Council on the Aging to ask for suggestions as to how you and your group can help the elderly.[3]

(16) Write the American Association of Retired Persons and the National Retired Teachers Association to find out what work they are doing that you might be a part of.[4]

(17) Subscribe to the "Older Americans in ACTION" newsletter.[5]

3
CORRECTIONAL REFORM

I'm like a dog who has gone through the K-9 process.

George Jackson
*Soledad Brother: The Prison
Letters of George Jackson*

I. Introduction

My personal interest in what I used to refer to as "prison reform" began seven years ago when I read *I Chose Prison* by James V. Bennett, Director of the Federal Bureau of Prisons under F.D.R. I changed my terminology to "correctional reform" when I discovered that the prison system was only one part of a complexity of ways by which our society "takes care of" those who break the rules. Correctional reform is an umbrella under which we find federal and state prisons, county and city jails, detention homes for youthful offenders, probation and parole systems, law enforcement agencies, etc. The correctional complex is a blood brother of the judicial complex, the latter frequently feeding the tragic shortcomings of the former.

Correctional efforts in this country do focus in large part on jails. The theory behind our present prison system is that to separate an offender for "X" number of years from the rest of society and enclose him in an environment threatening to his physical, mental and spiritual life will magically "cure" him of whatever it was that caused him to commit a crime. It just ain't so. For example, at the time of this writing, "more than 230 sex offenders, including child molesters, rapists and other deviates are serving prison terms in Oklahoma's prisons. Most of them will be returned to society . . . without ever receiving any psychological or psychiatric help. . . . 'We simply lock them up for a while . . . and then we put them right back on the streets again.' "[1] A single institution cannot both punish and cure. We are experts at punishing; we seemingly know nothing about healing.

Nearly one hundred years ago a convention of leading penologists and corrections officials met in Philadelphia and adopted thirty-three principles that would guide prison reform in the United States. The major ones were:

(1) The best legal and psychiatric knowledge should be em-

ployed to differentiate the mentally sick from the criminally responsible.

(2) Repeated short sentences imposed for recurring misdemeanors or petty offenses are ineffective, both as a means of correction and as a punitive deterrent.

(3) The architecture and construction of penal and correctional institutions should be functionally related to the programs to be carried on in them.

(4) Correctional workers need special professional education and training of a high standard.

(5) The goal of rehabilitation will be best achieved by individualized treatment of the offender.

(6) The offender should be sentenced on the basis of full consideration of the social and personality factors of the individual.

(7) The prisoner should receive the generally accepted standards of decent living and decent human relations. Their food, clothing and shelter should not be allowed to fall below the generally accepted standards.

(8) Rewards for conformance to the highest values of our culture should be given precedence over fear of punishment in guiding the development of human character in correctional systems.

(9) No law, procedure or system of correction should deprive any offender of the hope and the possibility of his ultimate return to full, responsible membership in society.

(10) Moral forces, organized persuasion and scientific treatment should be relied upon in the control and management of offenders, with as little reliance on physical force as possible.

(11) Every effort should be made to raise the educational and vocational skills of offenders.

(12) To hold employable offenders in correctional institutions without the opportunity to engage in productive work is to violate one of the essential objectives of rehabilitation.

(13) Psychiatric services should be provided to those offenders and prisoners who are abnormal.

(14) Suitable employment for a discharged offender is a major

factor in his rehabilitation and the regaining of his position
in society.

(15) With few exceptions offenders should be released under
parole supervision.

(16) The correctional process has as its aim the reincorporation
of the offender into the society as a normal citizen. . . .
Constructive community contacts should be encouraged.
The success of the correctional process . . . can be greatly
enhanced by energetic, resourceful and organized citizen
participation.[2]

An analyst of the prison situation some one hundred years
later prompted this list of present ills of American prisons:

(1) inadequate funding
(2) overcrowding of inmates
(3) poorly trained and poorly paid guards
(4) inadequate number of professional personnel
(5) haphazard and superficial parole procedures
(6) inadequate and poor food
(7) limited opportunities for constructive work and recreation
(8) inadequate educational opportunities
(9) long imprisonment without trial
(10) homosexuality, drug addiction, and crime among inmates
(11) brutal punishment for infraction of rules
(12) racial tension[3]

The reader can draw his or her own conclusions about the
gains made in the last century.

Inmates of correctional institutions (like mental patients)
have no lobby. They cannot vote in elections. Any interest
shown in their problems in the last one hundred years has as its
source sheer altruism. There is not a surplus of that commodity
in the United States at present. In addition, the majority of citizens see crime and the criminal as outside society, as enemies of
society in a "them against us" scenario. "This orientation leads

us to compartmentalize crime problems and to ignore their close relation to other conditions of society that produce both criminals and non-criminals."[4] (Is it some mammoth coincidence that the predominance of the 1.33 million souls in the complex of juvenile detention homes, city and county jails, federal and state penitentiaries are black, young, unemployed and from large cities?[5])

Crime is part of our society, interwoven with our values and institutions. To get at the conditions of society that produce criminals we must deal with questions at the very core of American political and economic life. We must critically assess and call to question every value and every institution which dehumanizes. In addition we must serve the immediate needs of those oppressed. Later in this chapter and throughout this book this two-pronged approach to social action will be repeated:
(1) Serve the needs of people.
(2) Change the structural barriers.

In researching the statistics of correctional facilities I assumed the first place I should look for the most up-to-date information was *The 1976 Almanac and Book of Facts.* Besides a brief reference to the trial resulting from the events at New York's Attica prison in 1971, the only reference to our correctional system in the entire 984-page tome was a brief listing of the locations of federal detention areas. This reference did not even include zip codes! Apparently Americans would rather dwell on information about their favorite baseball teams than upon others who are in need of healing. (Every conceivable statistic on every conceivable sport covers almost *one hundred pages* of the almanac, including full addresses of all major teams. Enough said about national religion.)

Since four out of every five crimes are committed by ex-offenders,[6] by those who have been through our corrections system at some level, the crime rate is directly related to the state of our correctional efforts. In other words our system is producing crime rather than reducing it. Presenting the following statistics on crime and its growth will put our correction needs in perspective. Beyond altruism our reform efforts realistically could come from a desire to survive as a society.

There is a violent crime (murder, forcible rape, robbery or assault to kill) committed once every thirty-three seconds. There is a serious crime committed nineteen times each minute. To further break these down, there is a burglary every ten seconds, a murder every twenty-six minutes, larceny theft every six seconds and a forcible rape every ten minutes in the United States.[7] During the period 1969 through 1974 per 100,000 inhabitants, the rate of burglaries rose 46%,[8] murders 33%,[9] and forcible rapes 42%.[10]

Most of these crimes are committed by youth. On any given day 30% of all offenders (350,000 kids) are under the custody or supervision of juvenile correction institutions or agencies.[11]

If our correctional system were working these figures should be going down, not up. We are not reducing crime or "curing" criminals through our present system but doing the exact opposite. We are encouraging crime and making better criminals.

What do these crime breeding institutions cost us? Our archaic prison institutions cost 27 million dollars per year—a figure which does not include costs related to this human misery.[12] This total cost of keeping an adult offender in a state institution is about six times as great as keeping him under parole supervision. It takes $11,000 per year to keep a married man in prison. The cost of that man on probation or parole averages less than $365 per year as reported by the President's Commission on Law Enforcement and the Administration of Justice.[13] What we do with the persons who commit crimes is central to the very survival of our society. Maintaining the present correctional system is a losing proposition for all members of the society.

As much as people talk about rehabilitation and mental health services for prisoners, there were in 1972 only twenty psychiatrists available for the entire federal corrections systems.[14] The budget for prisons is the first money cut from the proposed Justice Department budget each year. When Congress reviewed the Manpower Development Training Act program for budget savings in 1968, the first cut was for prisoner training and it was a 100% cut.[15] If there is to be hope that an ex-prisoner will not return to crime it is naive and short-sighted of us not to help find these persons meaningful employment upon their release as well as during their terms.[16]

In terms of the present state of probation and parole, the recommended caseload of a probation officer is thirty-five or less. Yet less than 4% of the probation officers in the U.S. carry a caseload of forty or less. The majority of those convicted of both major and minor offenses are on probation in caseloads of one hundred or more![17]

If prisons are not working, what will work? Many authorities on the subject say that community correction is a cheaper and more humane approach. Community correction means working with the offender in or near his home community. Specific community-based alternatives to prison are:
(1) pre-trial intervention
(2) probation
(3) halfway houses
(4) work release
(5) pre-release centers
(6) parole[18]

For youthful offenders a voluntary alternative in many areas is the Youth Service Bureau. These bureaus are resource centers for delinquent and non-delinquent youth which offer counseling and other concrete assistance, be it tutoring, supervised work experience, temporary residence, etc.

Many suggested actions to finding alternatives to the present correctional system as well as offering immediate aid to those involved are offered later in this chapter. The basis of any reform in this area is self-education and education of others in your community about the problem. This begins with individual and group study. A bibliography follows which should be required reading for anyone interested in reforming our correctional system. Keep in mind that on this particular work depends the very survival of our society. Any efforts you or your group make in this area help stunt the growth of the cancer called violence. The best anti-violence strategy is a massive individual and group effort for social justice.

II. Study Bibliography

Buckley, Marie. *Breaking Into Prison: A Citizen Guide To Volunteer Action*. Beacon Press: 1976.

Compendium of Model Correctional Legislation and Standards, American Bar Association.

Criminal Justice Newsletter (bi-weekly report from the National Council on Crime and Delinquency, 411 Hackensack Avenue, Hackensack, N.J. 07601, gives an idea of citizen involvement).

Jackson, George. *Soledad Brother: The Prison Letters of George Jackson*. Coward-McCann & Bantam Book, Inc.: New York, 1970.

Leinwand, Gerald (ed.). *Prisons*. Pocket Books: New York, 1972.

Menninger, Karl. *The Crime of Punishment*. Viking: New York, 1968.

Mitford, Jessica. *Kind and Usual Punishment: The Prison Business*. Knopf: New York, 1973.

Perlstein, Gary R. and Phelps, Thomas R. (eds.). *Alternatives to Prison: Community-Based Corrections*. Goodyear Publishing Co., Inc.: Pacific Palisades, California, 1975.

The Rights of Prisoners, ACLU Handbook.

III. Reflections as a Christian

As Christians our concern is with the basic human rights of all persons. When Jesus made the statements about ministering to those imprisoned (Mt. 25) he was preaching about the divinity within us all. "When I was in prison, you visited me" (Mt. 25:36). If we fail to see those behind bars as fellow partakers of the divinity it is little wonder we support the subhuman treat-

ment of them, either by virtue of our silence or by our protract-
ed ignorance. As disciples of Christ we must join him in his mission "to bring good news to the poor, to proclaim liberty to
captives, and freedom to prisoners" (Lk. 4:18, Is. 61:1).

The present system of criminal justice is Old Testament in
genre. Grace and law have two different meanings in the Old
Testament and the New Testament. God was seen in Old Testament times as vengeful; his justice was based on an eye-for-
an-eye type of contract. When television's "Maude" says, "God
is going to get you for that, Walter," she is talking of God as
the Old Testament people (as well as many holdovers in our
time) perceived him.

The present corrections system reflects the idea many have
of this vengeful God. A society which has not heard the Good
News (or, as Morton Kelsey has said, sees the Good News as
merely the Good Advice) has no room for healings. It is a
society comfortable with the politician's statement about how
to handle those who had wronged him: "Don't get mad; get
even."

The God of the New Testament acts like a person crazy in
love with mankind, paying all the same wage although not all
had labored the full day. The New Testament God is a person
in love with late bloomers as well as early risers. His justice is
wrapped in a total love gift. His laws are made for mankind.
Those who break his laws even seventy times seven have hope of
forgiveness and healing.

Mahatma Gandhi had a word for the stance Jesus took
when others wronged him—"satyagraha." "Satyagraha is the
vindication of truth not by infliction of suffering on the opponent
but on one's self. The opponent must be weaned from error by
patience and sympathy. Weaned, not crushed. Satyagraha re-
verses the eye-for-an-eye-for-an-eye-for-an-eye policy which
ends in making everybody blind or blind with fury. It returns
good for evil until the evildoer tires of evil. . . . An implicit
trust in human nature is the very essence of (this) creed" (*Gandhi*, by Louis Fischer).

As partakers of the *New* Covenant are we more concerned
with healing and reconciling than with "getting even"?

Our ways of correcting not only are dehumanizing to those

inside prison walls but, like all oppression, they are more dehumanizing to the keepers of the keys. Through prayer, study and reflection leading to organized action we will know the truth about this abridgement of human rights to healing growth, and, in Luke's words, the truth shall set us (all) free.

Scripture Passages for Reflection

Matthew 25:31-46 (whatever you do to the least of my brethren)
Luke 17:4 (on brotherly correction)
Luke 22:47—23:46 (Jesus' own arrest, trial and execution)
Isaiah 61:1, 2
Matthew 5:38-42; 7:12
Matthew 7:1-5

IV. Questions for Reflection/Discussion

(1) To be a Christian is to be pro-life. If we are pro-life we are pro fostering independence, creativity, and self-determination in others. How does the prison system you have studied do this/fail to do this?

(2) The prison setting of today is without quiet and without privacy. What effect does this have on personal growth?

(3) What is meant by the phrase "my brother's keeper"?

(4) What as individual Christians and as a group do we have to say about the abolition of capital punishment?

(5) "The broken men (released from prison) are so damaged that they will never again be suitable members of any sort of social unit. Everything that was still good when they entered the joint . . . anything that may have been redeemable when they first entered the joint—is gone when they leave" (George Jackson, *Soledad Brother: The Prison Letters of George Jackson*). In this statement, what sin against the Holy Spirit is George Jackson describing?

(6) The most immediate and basic task of the Christian community is healing. How can I and my group minister to the correctional establishment in an organized way?

V. Suggested Actions

(1)   Form study group on this topic. Choose a book from the study bibliography, read it and discuss its implications.
(2)   Invite inmates to speak to groups to which you belong.
(3)   Invite ex-inmates to speak to groups to which you belong.
(4)   Volunteer at a prison or city or county jail to help with evening vocational programs for inmates.
(5)   Organize volunteers to participate in tutoring programs for the incarcerated.
(6)   Initiate a volunteer probation aid program to provide troubled youth with adult guidance and assistance with school work and finding jobs.
(7)   Hire (or start programs which encourage businesspeople to hire) ex-inmates to do meaningful jobs.
(8)   Initiate a program to provide persons in institutions periodic contacts with people from the community who can listen to their problems, advise them, and even develop special programs to take institutionalized offenders into their homes and into the community on a well-organized basis.
(9)   As an individual or with a group effort, contribute good books to prison libraries (a particular need stated by inmates is for better law libraries). Contact prison librarians —they welcome new books.
(10) Visit correctional institutions.
(11) Get together a group which raises bail money for offenders.[1]
(12) Found a halfway house where inmates can live after their release.[2]
(13) Support establishment of halfway houses and undertake a program to educate the community to the need for these facilities.
(14) Stimulate the development of detoxification centers to divert alcoholic offenders out of the correctional system and into facilities with medical services.
(15) Collect relevant research or information on the subject of corrections and correctional reform and reprint it in easily understood and readable form.

(16) Start a newsletter on correctional reform for your parish, neighborhood or other community.

(17) Use television and radio to encourage others to join in the correctional reform work (stations have free public access time—call them).

(18) Call juvenile court and ask for the coordinator of volunteers. Volunteer for clerical work, light counseling, getting jobs for children in trouble, obtaining volunteer professional services for children in trouble (eye exams, medical checkups, dental work, professional counseling, etc.), meeting their immediate physical needs.

(19) Advocate for the offender a link to community service agencies.

(20) Do what you can to redefine the role of probation and parole officer as community organizer.

(21) Support improvement and innovation in existing local correctional services.

(22) Support surveys of correctional facilities and services in terms of personnel requirements, standards for public buildings, food, sanitary conditions, treatment of prisoners, rehabilitation services, etc.

(23) Mobilize public and legislative support for diversified treatments and alternatives to incarceration.[3]

Addenda to Suggested Action List

I. In a *Blueprint for the Christian Reshaping of Society* the New Orleans Province Institute of Social Order urged the Assistancy of North American Jesuits to give immediate and full support to:

(1) the immediate decriminalization of victimless crimes;

(2) the abolition of capital punishment;

(3) programs of alternatives to correction:

  a. particularly immediate decentralization of the correction system;

  b. financial support for increased programs of delinquency control and youthful offenders;

  c. increased use of community-based facilities and community responsibility for such decentralized programs;

d. all possible support for the victims of crime;

e. reform of present sentencing practices: for example, restitution and not incarceration for property crimes, low maximum sentence for any crime;

(4) increased rights of inmates to freely choose or refuse legal, medical, psychological, and social assistance;

(5) the immediate moratorium on any further expansion of correctional facilities;

(6) increased community surveillance of all aspects of the criminal justice system;

(7) all sentences should be subject to review and open to commutation and parole.[4]

II. Lists are available of organizations in your state which would welcome volunteers.[5]

4

DRUGS AND ADDICTION

The use of . . . drugs is enmeshed in social ritual.

John A. Clausen
Contemporary Social Problems

I. Introduction

This section will be divided into five segments and will include brief answers to the following questions: What is drug addiction? What are some of the drugs which are being used and abused? How many people use and abuse drugs in our country? Why do people use and abuse them? What might some objectives be in meeting the drug problem?

Addiction refers to a condition brought about by the repeated administration of any drug "such that continued use of the drug is necessary to maintain normal physiological function, and discontinuance of the drug results in definite physical and mental symptoms."[1] Another expert puts it this way: "If you are using alcohol or drugs harmfully, and if you can't stop and stay stopped even when you seriously want to, you are addicted."[2]

It is possible to be only psychologically addicted to a drug because not all drugs are productive of physiological dependence. (Nor do all have the effect of producing a tolerance in the body requiring larger and larger doses.) Marijuana, for example, is not physiologically addictive, but alcohol is. Cocaine is not physiologically addictive, but heroin is.

If a physiologically addictive drug has been overused, one can become physically dependent on it. If the drug is then discontinued, acute illness results. This illness is called abstinence syndrome, or withdrawal. The phrase "kick the habit" originated in the writhing, kicking, and shaking that accompanies withdrawal from certain addictive drugs.

The effects of drug abuse go far beyond the individual addict. Family life and interpersonal relationships are drastically altered. The addict may very well not be able to hold a job, and is a hazard behind the wheel of a car. Physically, he is literally killing himself. (I am speaking here of physiologically addictive drugs when abused. For example, alcohol can kill a person; marijuana cannot.)

What are some of the drugs? Drugs fall into four basic classifications:

a. all *depressants*—e.g., narcotics, barbiturates, hypno-seda-tives, tranquilizers, alcohol;
b. all *stimulants*—e.g., cocaine, dexedrine, diet pills, caffeine;
c. *hallucinogens*—e.g., LSD, STP, DMT, marijuana;
d. *inhalants*—e.g., vaporized chemicals such as glue, paint thin-ner, gasoline.

The common ways drugs enter the body are: capsule or tablet, liquid, injectible solutions, intravenous or intramuscular, suppository, vapor by inhalation.[3]

The most abused drug in our society is alcohol, a depres-sant. It is addictive physiologically. Alcoholism is a disease which is never cured but can be controlled or arrested. Problem drinkers are found at all levels of social class and in all areas of our country. Of the 50,000 persons killed in traffic accidents yearly in our country, 50% of the accidents involve substantial blood alcohol levels in either the driver or the victim.[4]

Two out of every three of the adults in the United States drink. Many do not abuse the drink. It is estimated, however, that one out of every fifteen young people will eventually be-come an alcoholic.[5]

The very best way that I have found to learn about al-coholism is to call Alcoholics Anonymous and ask to have an AA member come to speak to your group. You will find the ex-perience the most instructive imaginable concerning what you can do to help alcoholics and to contribute to the fight against alcoholism.

In addition to alcohol some of the more common depres-sants are the barbiturates, Nembutal, Seconal, Luminal, Amy-tal, and Tuinal. The fastest acting of these are Nembutal and Seconal. They, therefore, are the most abused. The more famil-iar tranquilizers are Equanil, Miltown, Librium, and Valium.

The more common narcotic drugs are opiates such as opium, heroin, morphine, codeine, and paregoric. Heroin is syn-thesized from morphine though it is several times more power-ful. Several synthetic drugs are in the narcotics family—e.g., demerol and dolophine. (*N.B.* Cocaine and marijuana are *not* narcotics, but are classified as such *legally*.)

Medical uses for the depressant drugs are many. Doctors prescribe them to treat many conditions from high blood pressure to insomnia. As to the effects of high doses of depressants, the effects resemble alcoholic drunkenness: speech is slurred, the ability to work is impaired, the user appears confused and may become angry or want to become violent. Overdoses of depressants can cause death.

Stimulants pep one up, make one feel alert and self-confident. Examples of stimulants are cocaine, dexedrine, diet pills, and caffeine. Those who have taken high doses of stimulants appear withdrawn with dulled emotions, and they seem to be unable to organize their thinking.

Stimulants do not produce physical dependence as the narcotics do. The body does, however, become tolerant of these drugs, so larger and larger doses are needed to get the same effects. Abusing stimulants may cause psychological dependence. This means that the drug has become a habit for mental or emotional reasons with the person getting used to the drug or its effects.

Caffeine is a stimulant drug. It is found in coffee, tea, cocoa, and many soft drinks. It works directly on the brain. Nothing is known yet as to whether it is addictive or not, but my guess is that you can name many who are psychologically addicted to that cup of coffee or afternoon coke. Caffeine does constrict the vessels in the brain, thus frequently causing throbbing headaches.

In addition to those listed earlier, other hallucinogens are peyote, mescaline, psulocybin, and Morning Glory seeds. Hashish is, like marijuana, prepared from the flowering tops of the hemp plant but is many times more powerful than marijuana. Marijuana is classified as a mild hallucinogen. Its long-term effects are not known. It does not cause physical dependence as do the opiates, alcohol, and certain other drugs, and the body probably does not develop a tolerance to the drug. Withdrawal from marijuana does not produce physical sickness. A number of scientists think marijuana can cause psychological dependence, but much more study is needed.

LSD is an extremely potent hallucinogen. Its many dangers include panic, paranoia, and accidental death due to the feeling of invincibility or the feeling one has the ability to fly or float.

The inhalants are cardiac depressants. Some inhalants, in addition to those mentioned earlier, are nail polish and nail polish remover, lighter fluid, freon, and kerosene.

How many people use drugs? Here are some sample statistics of the reported experience with drug *use* for recreational and non-medical purposes by American youth and adults (all over twelve years of age) based on a 1972 survey:

alcoholic beverages (within the last 7 days) approximately 80,000,000 (a 1974 figure cites 95,000,000);[6]

tobacco, cigarettes[7] (within the last 7 days) approximately 58,000,000;

LSD, other hallucinogens (excluding marijuana) approximately 7,600,000;

heroin, approximately 2,000,000.[8]

For examples of the figures of those who *abuse* drugs let's look at the figures for alcohol and heroin. How many persons abuse alcohol in our country? Estimates run to approximately 10,000,000. A 1974 Gallup poll showed nearly one out of every four persons conceded that he sometimes drinks too much. It was also found in the same poll that one out of every eight persons said liquor was a source of trouble in his or her family.[9]

As for heroin, 100,000 persons in this country live chained to it. Others say the figure is close to 250,000.[10] Not all heroin users are addicts because it takes time to become addicted to the drug.

Why do people use and abuse drugs? Some reasons are: for health reasons, for relaxation, to combat fatigue, for a pick-up, to reduce inhibitions in social situations, to sleep, for fun, because of bad parental example of drug use, to face normal adolescent problems, to escape, because of boredom, because it is the fad, because they are anxious, because of psychosis/neurosis, to cope with sexual anxieties, to be "sociable," etc. In general, loneliness and alienation play a big part in drinking and taking other drugs. For the addict, the drug is necessary as a source of euphoria as well as a means of keeping the searing pains of withdrawal at bay.

What might some objectives be in meeting the drug abuse problem? Experts tell us that we must at the outset remove the moral tone from our approaches and substitute for it the possibility of good treatment. We need a shift from punishment to treatment and from condemnation to treatment. There is, by the way, no evidence that extreme penalties deter people from abusing or using drugs.[11]

The major objectives of this treatment should be:

(1) terminating physiological dependence through the withdrawal of the drug with a minimum of suffering;

(2) providing appropriate forms of therapy and training to increase the addict's personal resources so that he will subsequently not relapse or retreat to drug use.[12]

We need to be more discriminating in our categorizing of drugs and their effects, especially when making laws concerning their use. The National Commission on Marijuana and Drug Abuse said in March 1973:

> The experimental, recreational or circumstantial user of drugs is generally not more "sick" than the social drinker. . . . It becomes an absurdity to talk of treating such a person. . . . The most serious concern in contemporary America should attach to the use of alcohol and heroin. Moderate social concern should attach to the use of amphetamines, barbiturates, hallucinogens, methaqualone and cocaine, the use of which is relatively controlled. . . . The use of marijuana and the so-called minor tranquilizers appears to require relatively minimum social concern at the present time. Present trends do suggest, however, that the incidence and use of and dependence on barbiturates and cocaine may be increasing and may demand increased social attention.[13]

A friend who has been a professional in the field of drug treatment, John Boyle, put these emphases in regard to the problem of addiction:

> I hold that the class of drug addicts is the most discriminated against class in our society:
> 1. They are ripped off by the dealers in drug traffic.
> 2. They are arrested as criminals for only seeking the answer to one of their needs. An addict needs drugs.
> 3. Drug addicts have been convinced they are really social outcasts.
>
> Public policy about drug addiction is absurd, to say the least. The book *Licit and Illicit Drugs* deals with the question of public policy. A Christian could work toward a more sane and humane public policy toward drug addicts and drug abusers.
>
> There are openings for professionals and para-professionals in the treatment system. The work is demanding and offers few experiences of success. The most basic qualification would be a radical awareness of the value of a human existence, in spite of all the addict may do to deny that value.
>
> In the area of prevention of drug abuse among young people, the best tactic is not to talk about drugs, but deal with values clarification, ego development, and alternative life styles . . . or getting high without drugs.

II. Study Bibliography

Brecher, Edward M. and the Editors of *Consumer Reports. Licit and Illicit Drugs.* The Consumers' Union Report on Narcotics, Stimulants, Depressants, Inhalants, Hallucinogens, and Marijuana—Including Caffeine, Nicotine, and Alcohol. Little, Brown and Co.: Boston, 1972.

DeWitt, James, M.D. with Al Hirshberg. *Addict: A Doctor's Odyssey.* Cowles Book Co.: Chicago, 1972.

Silverstein, Alvin and Silverstein, Virginia. *Alcoholism.* J. B. Lippincott Co.: Philadelphia and New York, 1975.

III. Reflections as a Christian

The way much of our society treats the drug abuser suggests a basically un-Christian view of the nature of man and the important place of pleasure in our lives. One author puts it this way:

> In a culture committed to hard work, competition, aggressiveness, sequential thought, and postponed pleasure, the passivity, pleasure, and escape from discursive thought provided by drugs seem wrong. Likewise, where independence and the self-made man are ideals, it seems destructive, or at best unfair, to find happiness, pleasure, and insight artificially, without the industry that usually precedes and lends such states value. The strictness of the standard, which like Victorian sexual mores condemns a single departure, implies a view of man as innately evil. So strong are man's desires, and so vulnerable the wall he erects against his evil instincts, that once the forbidden fruits are tasted, he will fall prey to his appetites. Thus, one shot makes an addict, and one marijuana cigarette often is thought to cause personality disintegration.
>
> The strength of these feelings was evident in the reasoning of the lower court in the Leis case, which found marijuana to be harmful because, among other things, it causes "a euphoric and unreal feeling of exhilaration and an abnormally subjective concentration on trivia" and leads "the user to lose perspective and focus his attention on one object to the exclusion of all others." Such reasoning does not spring from a rational assessment of tangible injury to user or others. It

rests on a subjective feeling that pleasure, contemplation, and inactivity for their own sake cannot be worthwhile, and are thus wrong.[1]

The laws our society has enacted and the attitudes our society propagates toward those who abuse drugs imply our mistrust of the goodness of man. These attitudes will short-circuit our truly being able to help the addict because they imply a dwarfed awareness of the value of human life.

For the Christian, man is basically a good creature, created in the divine image. Christians do not view mankind as weak and unable to enjoy both pleasure and work in balanced amounts. If we did, we could not possibly believe that God is all-forgiving and that the Kingdom will indeed be fulfilled.

God made us good. He made us to take pleasure in his earth. Pleasure, recreation, and inactivity are good for the soul. On the subject of temperance, one author has this to say:

> The Christian's critical question is not the legitimacy of pleasure or enjoyment, but rather, the coordination of pleasure with the other goals of human life. . . . Pleasure is . . . appropriate when it reinforces rather than impedes his quest for self-transcendence. . . . [We] must be able to enjoy the surging waters of the lake, the never-ending fascinations of Andre Malraux's invisible museum, exercise, conversation, games (and not merely those to be observed in the picture tube), vacations, laughter, good food, good wine, and good sex. To the extent that [we] cannot do so, we must be classified both an intemperate and un-Christian.[2]

Finally, in terms of helping those who are addicts, it is the role of the Christian to heal rather than condemn. Christians must be sons of the light and of the day—both in their individual use of drugs and in their loving witness to others concerning *the* natural high, Jesus.

Scripture Passages for Reflection

Matthew 11:28-30
2 Corinthians 12:9-10
1 Thessalonians 5:4-8
John 9:4-5
Luke 10:36-37

IV. Questions for Reflection/Discussion

(1) What is the meaning of this chapter's introductory quote: "The use of . . . drugs is enmeshed in social ritual"?

(2) What crucial meaning is behind the use of the phrase *"recovered* addict" rather than *"reformed* addict"?

(3) What drugs do you and those in your group use regularly? (Answer individually.)

(4) What are two things you are looking for in your use of drugs?

(5) What are five things heavy drug users might be seeking?

(6) What can your group do to enable the drug abusers in your community to find what they are seeking?

V. Suggested Actions

(1) Become informed about drugs through reading the references in the study bibliography and by inviting an alcoholic or other addict to speak to your group.[1]

(2) Check with your local drug treatment agencies to see if you can assist them in establishing or staffing detoxification centers, rap centers, crash pads, crisis intervention centers, drug hot lines, and free clinics.

(3) Support development of special treatment programs in your city, county and state jails for addicts.

(4) Offer your assistance to schools in providing drug education to the students. This could be done through the PTA.

(5) Procure films for drug education programs. The Regional Offices of the Bureau of Narcotics and Dangerous Drugs will loan certain films free to civic organizations. Metropolitan libraries are a good source also.

(6) Contribute materials to your local radio and television stations' research libraries on the topic of drugs and drug abuse.

(7) Put together or borrow a pre-existing drug display and arrange to show it at banks, office buildings, libraries, schools, clinics, etc. Local merchants, pharmacists, and physicians might donate free space.

(8) Write the Publications Division, National Council on Alcoholism, Inc., 2 Park Avenue, New York, N.Y. 10016 for information about alcohol and its abuse.

(9) Write the National Clearinghouse for Drug Abuse Information, 5454 Wisconsin Ave., Chevy Chase, Md. 20015 for materials.

(10) For guidelines on requesting monetary support for your activities, write The Bureau of Narcotics and Dangerous Drugs, Prevention Programs Division, 1405 Eye St., N.W., Washington, D.C. 20537.

(11) Support any public policy or legislation which focuses on *treatment* of drug abusers.

5
ENVIRONMENT

A dead ocean means a dead planet.

Thor Heyerdahl

I. Introduction

There is a limit to all resources. Our planet, like our back yard garden, has limited dimensions and production capacities. In the past and still today we live with the misconception that the atmosphere is boundless, the sea is boundless, and the earth is limitless in its production possibilities. We are dead wrong.

Our survival, our health, and welfare depend on this complex system of interacting facets. No approach to environmental improvement makes sense if we talk only of one aspect of the total ecosystem. Any tampering we do with any ecological problem, be it air, noise, water, or other pollution, will have a chain reaction on every segment of the ecosphere. Experts tell us that "the social, physical, and biological components function as an integrated system, and any tampering with any part of the system will affect each of the other parts and alter the whole."[1]

To appreciate the complexity of the environment in which we live we have only to look at the table of contents of a book on the subject. Chapter headings will include: Insecticides, Sanitary Sewage, Water Pollution, Air Pollution, Solid-Waste Disposal, Accidents, Noise, Occupational Health, Ionizing Radiation, Biological and Chemical Warfare, Zoonoses: Diseases of Animals Transmissible to Man, Chemicals in Food, Bacterial Food Poisoning, Ecology of Health and Disease.[2]

Items

(1) The relatively thin layer of air which stretches from the surface of the earth toward outer space is some five to eleven miles deep. It is the room in which we live. This windowless room contains the air we breathe and the air we pollute. As of 1970 the annual amount of aerial garbage poured into the air above our cities was estimated at from 125 to 150 million tons —a greater tonnage than our annual steel production.[3] We are becoming accustomed to yellow alerts in our larger cities—days when it is lethal for some to breathe the air outside.

(2) Each year throughout our country we must dispose of forty-eight billion cans, twenty-six billion bottles and jars, and sixty-five million metal and plastic caps. In New York City alone five million tons of garbage and refuse are collected yearly. What new places can we find and what new ways can we devise for disposing of the billions of tons of solid waste (cartons, boxes, paper, grass, plastics, bedding, clothing, ashes, cans, crockery, metal furniture, glass, bathtubs, wastes from food growing, preparation, and cooking, market wastes, dead animals, bricks, masonry, piping, lumber, septic tank sludge, junked automobiles, solids from the coarse screening of domestic sewage) we generate each year?[4]

(3) Our oceans are really big lakes which are landlocked on all sides. They are dead ends, the place where the buck stops in terms of pollution. Only pure water evaporates into the clouds so the oceans are the Final Garbage/Chemical/Waste Dump. Although oceans cover 71% of the earth they are remarkably shallow for their size. Marine life is concentrated in only about four percent of the oceans total body of water. The other ninety-six percent is very poor in life. Less than one-half of one percent of the ocean space represents the home of ninety percent of all marine life. This marine life is concentrated in the shallow coastal waters, the same coastal waters which receive sewer outlets and the water from polluted river mouths as well as silt from chemically treated farmland.[5] Groups within our society are showing active concern in matters of water and the life it supports.[6]

Why is the pollution of the environment a problem for our age more than any in the past? In the grand design of earth, nothing was composed by nature that could not be recomposed, recycled, and used again in another form. Man in our own era has sidetracked nature. As Thor Heyerdahl puts it:

> We put atoms together into molecules of types nature had carefully avoided. We invent to our delight immediately useful materials like plastics, pesticides, detergents, and other chemical products hitherto unavailable on planet earth. . . . Most of our new chemical

products are not only toxic: they are in fact created to sterilize and kill. And they keep on displaying these same inherent abilities wherever they end up . . . they all head for the ocean. . . . If it had not been for the present generation, man could have gone on polluting the ocean forever with the degradable waste he produced.[7]

Much of the 1.3 *billion* pounds of pesticides produced in the world *annually* ends up in the oceans. Heyerdahl goes on to point out that a dead ocean means a dead planet.

What about conservation efforts? The Sierra Club tells us that it has taken a century to pull together a national park system in America of twenty-seven million acres, a system of wildlife refuges totalling thirty-two million acres, and a wilderness system of fifteen million acres. Now we face the urgent task of putting one hundred million acres or more of Alaska in these and other reserves. Conservationists argue that if we err in favor of conservation at least choices will remain open to us in the future. Land use decisions are made very slowly; the process of persuading public authorities to act is extremely slow.[8] Many groups including the Sierra Club are taking action in conservation of land and wildlife at the all-important legislative level.[9]

What about energy? Experts tell us that coal reserves in the earth at present estimates will only take us part-way into the next century. Should we go ahead with nuclear energy as a major energy resource? What are the possibilities of concentrating time and money on the development of energy from the oldest source, the sun? Can we in conscience "use up" that most popular of fossil fuels—oil? What will the coming generations substitute for lubricants and plastics and other petroleum products if we do? Communities in our country even now are being asked to vote on such questions.

We are all polluters, but Americans are *big* polluters. Pollution seems to increase as affluence increases. The fault lies with individuals, businesses, government, and others. No institution of our society is blameless.

Why haven't we come together on making an integrated effort at saving spaceship earth? In a recent interview on the state of the nation in the bicentennial year, historian Henry Steele Commager bemoaned the lack of a fiduciary interest at large. The now generation seems to be short-sighted in terms of what it will leave for posterity. As Theodore Roosevelt said:

> The nation behaves well if it treats the natural resources as assets which it must turn over to the next generation increased and not impaired in value.[10]

Our approaches must not be piecemeal. We must deal at the legislative level nationally and seek for worldwide legislation relating to the ecosystem. We must shift from fragmented to integrated approaches to pollution. We must seek coordination of diverse segments of our society (science, government, education, individuals), pooling our knowledge to plan for the future.

Some progress has been made. Within the past five years major environmental legislation has been passed including the Clean Air and Water Acts, Noise Control Act, Solid Waste Disposal and Resources Recovery Act, and the Safe Drinking Water Act. The job is far from complete.

A recent poll indicates that sixty percent of the total American public is willing to pay higher prices to protect the environment rather than run the risk of more pollution.[11] Yet this interest is not seen in many obvious efforts. In 1975 the use of recycled materials of all kinds plunged. Our present recycling rate is a low seventeen percent. In our country recycling is restricted by tax, transportation and purchasing policies which make it more profitable for U.S. industry to use virgin materials than recycled ones.[12] Congress is considering legislation to rectify at least some of this discrimination but a nationwide effort to appreciate the value of recycling is necessary.

In conclusion two points should be made. First, it cannot be stressed enough that we should take into account the larger ecosystem in treating a seemingly local problem. A solution to one environmental difficulty which seems adequate might very well be causing other even less desirable environmental hazards. For example, to burn refuse is a fine solution for the problem of not enough dumping space for garbage, but the burning increases the quantity of smoke and volatile chemicals in the air and contributes to air pollution.

Second, our environmental interests should be more than national in scope. In environmental concerns we should think in ever widening circles. Any action should be seen in the light of its effects planet-wide, and therefore any action taken will be most effective if it is international in breadth. This orientation demands of us an openness to regulatory agencies of a multi-national type as well as support from us for the concept of a special oneness of the entire human family.

II. Study Bibliography

Benarde, Melvin A. *Our Precarious Habitat: An Integrated Approach To Understanding Man's Effect on His Environment.* W. W. Norton & Co., Inc.: New York, 1970.

Heyerdahl, Thor. "How To Kill an Ocean." *Saturday Review*, November 29, 1975, pp. 12-18.

Sierra Club Bulletin. A subscription can be obtained by writing c/o P.O. Box 7959, Rincon Annex, San Francisco, Cal. 94120. The bulletin is "designed to keep you up-to-date on local, national and international news of concern to environmentalists."

Cousteau, Jacques-Yves. "The Pulse of the Sea," A Monthly Newsletter, *Saturday Review*. (This column will help keep you up-to-date with much that is of environmental concern.)

III. Reflections as a Christian

The nature of the Christian pilgrimage is one of temporariness. We can never really "own" a piece of land. We rent the earth and all its resources from God. And God, like the lover he is, requires no security deposit of us. (Can you imagine letting your home or room with all of its books, cherished mementos, living things and other valuables for free? Can you imagine asking no security deposit?)

Just as is true of the responsibility we have toward our children, friends, and fellow travelers, our tenant status on spaceship earth involves a sacred trust. Our history has not overwhelmingly shown us to be worthy of that trust. Jacques Cousteau reports on the man-made destruction of the environment through the ages:

- A great forest—the Sahara—was destroyed and turned into desert by nomads and shepherds 8,000 years ago.
- The idyllic Greek islands were stripped of their forests in order to build ships and to provide homes with firewood. They are now sterile rock.
- The Cape Verde Islands, completely bare today, were described by Bartholomeu Dias as a paradise.
- Europe's wolves, bears, rain forests, were exterminated.[1]

The list is long. Cousteau remarks that the same technology which has destroyed resources in the past has the means to reverse the trend:

Although the situation at the dawn of the industrial age, more than 200 years ago, was far less serious than it is today, it was hopeless because there was no technology available to reverse the trend. Yesterday our ancestors did not *know*, and they could not *do*. Today we *know*, and we *can*, but we *don't*.[2]

Because technology tells us we *can* have this or that, we think we *should* have it, regardless many times of the environmental consequences. Our technical capabilities inspire technology's basic moral question: If we *can,* does it automatically follow that we *should*? Greed, self-interest, lust for power and other possessions drive us onward toward what one of my former graduate theology professors calls the "piggy-hoggy" existence.

Contrary to all appearances, the earth and its riches do not exist for ourselves and our use on the short run. They exist for God for whom and through whom everything exists (Heb. 2:10).

The complex life chain of the earth and its inhabitants are God's and are to be cherished while being enjoyed. Cousteau says:

> It was the contemplation of life that inspired Father Teilhard de Chardin's dissertation on three infinities: in addition to the infinitely big and the infinitely small, Teilhard told us, there is also the infinitely complex— life. This is what we should all defend.[3]

If we now know how we can reverse the trend away from the senseless rape of the resources of God's earth and yet we do not act on this knowledge, we are defilers of the first order. Jesus would have nothing to do with us.

Scripture Passages for Reflection

Genesis 1, especially vv. 9, 11, 20, 24, 26, 29-31
Exodus 22:4-5
Colossians 1:15-17
Hebrews 2:10

IV. Questions for Reflection/Discussion

(1) What is meant by "dominion . . . over all the earth?"
(2) At what point do we draw the line in terms of not doing what we technically have the "know-how" to do?
(3) What effect, if any, does the profit motive have on the environment?
(4) What effect, if any, does emphasis on a spirit of nationalism have on the environment?

(5) Are noise and personal growth in Jesus compatible? To what degree?

(6) What responsibilities do I and my group have to the land, air, and water of my town, state, region, planet?

V. Suggested Actions

(1) Encourage your local schools, colleges, universities, businesses, and churches to specify the need for recycled fibers in their paper, paperboard, and stationery.

(2) Request your local supermarket chain stores and large department stores to specify the need for recycled fibers in the boxes and corrugated containers which bring their merchandise to them.

(3) Look for the recycling symbol on the individually identifiable shopping bags stores give away or sell.

(4) Buy products in recycled containers.

(5) Ask in stores for the names of the suppliers and/or manufacturers of products so that you and your group can write to them to urge the increased use of recycled fibers in packaging. Ask the store managers to write also.

(6) Bring your own (cloth) grocery bags to the store; use cloth instead of paper when beneficial to the environment.

(7) Discourage wasting paper; use both sides of paper.

(8) Take cans, bottles, and newspapers to appropriate reclamation centers.

(9) Start a glass, can, or paper reclamation center and make arrangements with appropriate industries to buy what you collect.

(10) Do not use colored (dyed) paper products if they will end up in the waters of the world (e.g., use white toilet paper).

(11) Use "biodegradable" soaps and detergents.

(12) Do not waste *anything* (wash it, paint it, reheat it, repair it).

(13) About being "fuelish"
  (a) turn off lights you are not using;

> (b) use clothes and dishwashers with full loads; try using cold water for clothes wash or rinse cycles;
> (c) carpool; use public transportation; walk; bike;
> (d) support mass transit;
> (e) if possible cut down on use of air conditioners in warm weather; keep thermostat down to 68° in cold weather;
> (f) observe the 55 mph speed limit;
> (g) support legislation in your state for right hand turns at red lights;[1]
> (h) eliminate unnecessary electrical appliances;
> (i) do not idle your car while waiting for someone; do not delay in shifting gears (idling and revving the engine wastes fuel);
> (j) build houses and support housing codes which make the best use of energy (e.g., roof overhang in hot climates).

(14) Educate your group, parish, and community to responsibility for the environment through newsletters, speakers, audio-visual programs, leafletting, etc.

(15) With your group clean up any section of your neighborhood—a park, a beach, a stretch of highway, etc.

(16) The youth of your group could initiate a paper drive.

(17) Do not burn leaves; do not throw away grass cuttings.

(18) Make your own fertilizer from organic waste products (there are many good books in your local library with specifics on composting, mulching, and so forth).

(19) Buy products with the least wasteful packaging; where sanitary, reuse store packaging.

(20) Do not burn trash in inefficient home incinerators.

(21) Open dumping must be discontinued. Dumping in the waterways must be discontinued. Study alternatives (like sanitary landfill) and support their implementation.

(22) Encourage groups, individuals, philanthropists, and private foundations to set funds aside for cleaner water. (Why have only libraries and such been named after public officials? How about waste treatment plants?)

(23) You and your group raise funds for environmental concerns. Remember environmental needs in your will.

(24) Educate yourself and your group to nuclear, solar, and fossil energies, their implications and possibilities.

(25) Work for legislation which you and your group think has the whole planet in mind.

(26) Discourage insularity or the inability to think in terms of regional or overall schemes.

(27) Support waste-disposal research and development and support raising its status.

(28) Support a change in attitude as to the importance of engineers and scientists who are concerned with "low status" aspects of environment and health (e.g., solid waste disposal).

(29) Begin to act on the conviction that life in the urban setting can be a wholesome experience. Reflect on what your group can do to "make whole" or heal our urban areas.

6
HUNGER

**This little piggy had roast beef and
this little piggy had none.**

Children's Rhyme

I. Introduction

Hunger is a function of poverty. The subject of poverty is taken up in a later chapter.

I am confident that within a day's car drive at most (a drive of a few minutes at least) from most pockets of hunger and poverty in the world there is at least one restaurant in which the not so poor are being served a lobster or filet mignon dinner with the appropriate wine for each course.

It is a simple economic truth that if there are ten apples on the kitchen table and two people to eat them, if one person takes seven of them, the other will get only three. Just yesterday I received a reply from one of my United States Senators concerning my urging him to support S.Con.Res. 66—the "Right to Food" resolution (see end of introduction for text). The upshot of his reply was that in order for such a program to work, an effective means would need to be found to increase the world's food production. He is pessimistic about committing our energies to feed the world's hungry because he in effect says that we need *more* than ten apples to begin with. Never once in his letter did he indicate that the redistribution of the food which the world already produces might be a prior consideration. He never considered the fact that perhaps the one person taking seven of the ten apples might instead take only five. We are talking about *redistribution.* It is a commonly overlooked approach toward solving the world's hunger problems. One reason it is frequently de-emphasized is because it might mean one less lobster in the Senate dining room or denying oneself that extra slice of prime rib. We will discuss more about that orientation in part III of this chapter. Suffice it to say that it is the contention of many analysts that the difficult problem in feeding the world's hungry is in distributing food properly, not producing it.

Back to our apple analogy. With a certain amount of any good, if some have more, others have less. America is a "have more" country. With six percent of the world's population Americans consume forty percent of the world's goods. What is almost as shocking is that we had an agriculture secretary who said: "Why shouldn't we?"[1]

In our own food-ridden country distribution is a mighty problem. The Senate Select Committee on Nutrition and Human Needs in 1975 estimated that there were twenty million United States citizens eligible for food stamps not on the program.[2] There are many malnourished persons in our country. Most U.S. citizens who are hungry are white, although hunger is experienced by a higher *percentage* of blacks. Hunger is concentrated among the rural population, especially in the South and in Appalachia.[3] The segment of our society which suffers malnutrition most is native Americans.[4]

It is commonly known that malnourishment especially in pre-natal life and in early life can lead to mental retardation. Medical studies tell us that there is a correlation between good nutrition and good school work in children. I recall asking a young remedial reading and math tutee of mine on Homan Avenue in Chicago ten years ago what he had for breakfast before leaving for school in the mornings. He replied, "Nothin' or sometime' potato chips." It was a wonder he could concentrate at all when it came time to learn to read.

Experts estimate further that millions of tons of food go into the garbage pails of Americans each year as waste. (A friend once said to me as I was putting leftover spaghetti in a refrigerator container, "Oh, do you save leftover spaghetti? I just throw ours away. What could I do with it? My husband won't eat leftovers.")

There are 400 to 500 million hungry people in the world. Today the United States provides only 1/10th of the food aid it did ten years ago.[5] Few realize that the United States spends about one-fifth of *one* percent of its GNP on development assistance to the poor countries. It ranks near the *bottom* of industrialized countries when assistance is measured with income.[6] At the Rome Food Conference the United States made no serious commitment of its food reserves to the world's hungry. Yet during the period 1975-85 the U.S. Department of Agriculture projects a *surplus* of 51.9 million tons of grain for *developed* countries, a *deficit* of 47.6 million tons for *developing* countries.[7]

Science tells us that even with unlimited fossil energy the world's arable land is insufficient to feed the world's population of 4 billion a diet similar to that consumed in the U.S.[8] (It seems that is good in the long run for the world nutrition-wise. When Americans sent foods that we routinely eat as relief to Guatemala after the earthquake, much of what was contributed, boxed, and shipped was useless, since it was "too rich" for the stomachs of our neighbors to the south.)

The major lack in the diets of the malnourished is protein. Yet the rich minority of the world feeds as much grain (a major source of protein) to animals as the rest of the world eats. Our livestock consume grain and vegetable proteins to produce high quality animal protein. In addition half of the fish catch of the world goes to feed cattle. Eighteen million tons of protein is lost annually in America's eating of huge amounts of meat and poultry—enough to correct ninety percent of the world's protein deficiency.[9] We must divert protein fed to livestock (and housepets?) in order to balance the world's diet. U.S. per capita meat consumption is the highest in the world—in 1974 two hundred and fifty pounds per person. Primarily because we use *animal* protein as our major source of protein, the average U.S. citizen consumes about 1,850 pounds of grain per year, most of it in meat and dairy products, some as alcohol. The average in poorer countries is 400 pounds per person.[10]

When our family stopped consuming meat other friends asked, "How can you be sure you're getting the protein you need without relying on meat?" Here is the story on meat. Proteins are made up of amino acids. The body cannot make eight of the amino acids necessary for growth and maintenance. We must eat these in foods. There are two kinds of protein—complete and incomplete. A complete protein like meat gives you all eight essential amino acids. An incomplete protein is limited in one or more of the amino acids. So an incomplete protein eaten alone will not support life indefinitely. The lacking essential amino acids must be supplied by either a complete protein or by a *different* incomplete protein.

So if you are looking for meat substitutes look for complete proteins. These major protein sources, in addition to meat, are (Group 1): fish and poultry, cheese, milk in any form, and eggs. Remember that any complete protein will supplement the missing amino acids in an incomplete protein. So eating one serving from Group 1 with one serving from Group 2 will give you quite a lot of your amino acid needs. The incomplete proteins are (Group 2): legumes (beans, lentils, garbanzos), soy proteins (including commercial soy meat foods), and cereals-grains (breads, cereals, gluten-meat foods).

Usually two or more incomplete proteins from botanically different plant sources will supplement each other's lacking amino acids.[11] The easiest way we have found to eat the protein we need is to add some protein to every dish we eat.

The most important point to be made in this introduction is that eating no or less grain-fed meat will not feed the world's protein poor. This symbolic action must be combined with efforts at changing the profile of our government aid-to-the-hungry structures. In the same way personal fasting (see suggested actions) alone is not a complete action for feeding the stomachs of others. By itself fasting has witness value only. It must be combined with diverting money saved by fasting to the hungry as well as efforts toward major political and structural societal changes.

The Bread for the World organization[12] is an ecumenical group which works with changing governmental structures to alleviate hunger. "Without responsible politics in this area we turn our backs on hungry people."[13] Or more specifically, "Food will reach hungry people only if government policies see to its proper production and distribution, so an adjustment in eating habits without responsible citizenship may prescribe failure and hurt family farmers."[14]

So again there should be a two-pronged approach to our social action in this area. First we must meet the immediate needs of the hungry in our communities and around the world as best we can while, second, we change the social, economic, and political structures that encourage hunger and indeed profit from it.

Many of our governmental approaches to aid are tied to political and economic concessions given us by the needy countries in exchange for their birthright (see section III), that is, the products of the earth! Donations our government makes of fertilizer are made in the same way as food—they are tied to political objectives.

During the 1960's and early 1970's fifty million acres out of the total U.S. cropland base of three hundred and fifty million acres was held out of production to "support prices." Meanwhile food reserves dropped drastically. Most of this idled land was released in 1973 and the rest later, but food reserves have not been rebuilt.[15] The present situation is aimed at making profits, not feeding people.

I offer you three last points for your consideration. First, besides eating less grain-fed meat (which does not mean we could not switch to predominantly grass-fed meat) we must in general eat and consume less. Our country ranks number one in incidence of obesity and heart disease (and I suggest greed) among other over-consumption-related ailments.

Second, with a projected world population of seven billion in the year 2000 the most important area of needed action is in the area of population control. "Clearly if man does not control his numbers, nature will."[16]

Third, we must always and everywhere keep in mind that "the most fundamental and difficult part of the hunger question has to do with remedying the worst features of poverty."[17]

CONGRESSIONAL RECORD   *September 25, 1975*

RESOLUTION DECLARING AS NATIONAL POLICY THE RIGHT TO FOOD

House: H. Con. Res. 393
Senate: S. Con. Res. 66

Whereas an estimated 460 million persons, almost half of them young children, suffer from acute malnutrition because they lack even the calories to sustain normal human life; and

Whereas those who get enough calories but are seriously deficient of proteins or other essential nutrients may include half of the human race; and

Whereas the President, through his Secretary of State, proclaimed at the World Food Conference a bold objective for this nation in collaboration with other nations: "that within a decade no child will go to bed hungry, that no family will fear for its next day's bread, and that no human being's future and capacities will be stunted by malnutrition"; and

Whereas all the governments at the World Food Conference adopted this objective; and

Whereas in our interdependent world, hunger anywhere represents a threat to peace everywhere; and

Whereas the coming bicentennial provides a timely occasion to honor this nation's founding ideals of "liberty and justice for all," as well as our tradition of assisting those in need, by taking a clear stand on the critical issue of hunger: Now, therefore, be it

Resolved That it is the sense of the (Senate/House of Representatives) that

1. Every person in this country and throughout the world has the right to food—the right to a nutritionally adequate diet— and that this right is henceforth to be recognized as a cornerstone of U.S. policy; and

2. This right become a fundamental point of reference in the formation of legislation and administrative decisions in areas such as trade, assistance, monetary reform, military spending and all other matters that bear on hunger; and

3. Concerning hunger in the United States we seek to enroll on food assistance programs all who are in need, to improve those programs to insure that recipients receive an adequate diet, and to attain full employment and a floor of economic decency for everyone; and

4. Concerning global hunger this country increase its assistance for self-help development among the world's poorest people, especially in countries most seriously affected by hunger, with particular emphasis on increasing food production among the rural poor; and that development assistance and food assistance, including assistance given through private, voluntary agencies, increase over a period of years until such assistance has reached the target of one percent of our total national production (GNP).

II. Study Bibliography

Brown, Lester (with Erik Eckholm). *By Bread Alone*. Praeger Publishers: New York, 1974.
"Hunger." *Gamaliel*. Gamaliel: 1335 N Street, N.W., Washington, D.C. 20005, Volume 1, Number 1, Spring, 1975.
Simon, Arthur. *Bread for the World*. Paulist Press: New York, 1975.

III. Reflections as a Christian

I recall a night when we had relatives visiting and my husband got a call to pick up friends stranded two hours away. As he was leaving to pick them up we said, "Why don't you tell them to make other arrangements for the night and you'll pick them up at a more convenient time tomorrow morning?" Jim replied, "If we want to really help them it won't be by doing what *we* consider helpful, but what they consider helpful, and they asked me urgently to come now."

Jesus gave his life for us and suggested we too die for others by dying to ourselves. Many times the sacrifices we offer are on our terms, not his terms. It is less than going the extra mile if we do it on our terms and under conditions we set. For example, if we help feed the hungry with what remains after (and not until) our own stomachs are full, on whose terms are we helping them? Had Jesus used this approach he might have died in bed at the age of 75.

The hungry of the world have needs to be met, immediate and long-range. Their terms include that there will be less of the fat of the earth for our stomachs, less profit for the foodstuffs we produce, and a sharing of the hunger pains sometimes.

The commentary on hunger published by Gamaliel includes: "The year of Jubilee in Leviticus called for communal sharing to eliminate social inequalities as acknowledgment that God is the author and giver of all goods" (p. 48). To whom do the earth and its produce *really* belong?

When my son Nathaniel bangs his spoon on his high chair tray demanding food, I tell Jim that he is just demanding his birthright and "good for him!" Man's birthright is enough food, light, and air to grow to his potential. Good nutrition has been shown to have definite links to healthy mental development. But there is no flexing of muscles for the hungry, no reflecting of mind. There is no quiet. Survival is the name of the game and victories are won on a day-to-day basis. The starving literally haven't a prayer if they haven't some of our food.

But what of my own needs and the needs of my family? If I give my food away, what will I eat? The question is, do we believe what Jesus told us or don't we? Many people say: "I trust Jesus to take care of my needs, but. . . ." Jesus is the bread of life. If we trust in him and boldly dare to feed the world, it will be done. Point number one of Jesus' seven-point program is "Feed the hungry." To respond to this call we must start the work in our own homes and communities and legislatures.

Pray that it will be done. Read and reflect on the foregoing books in the study bibliography on this topic (section II). Act.

(As a first action your group might find helpful the worship aids from the Bread for the World organization which follow the final section of this chapter.)

Scripture Passages for Reflection

Matthew 6:25-33
Matthew 25:31-41

John 6:1-14
John 6:48-51
Exodus 16:1-12
Psalm 78:17-31
Isaiah 58:6-7

(For a lengthy list of Old and New Testament references see pp.
157-159 in Simon's *Bread for the World*.)

IV. Questions for Reflection/Discussion

(1) We are a world community, not a competing horde. To be a
    citizen of the planet first and my own country second is a
    Christian orientation. Do you agree with this statement?
    Why or why not? What implications might the statement
    have for our foreign and domestic policies regarding food-
    stuffs and their production and distribution?

(2) To be a Christian is to be sacrifice, yet most of us never feel
    hungry even for a moment. How do we reconcile these two
    facts? Should we reconcile them?

The following four questions are excerpted from the Arthur
Simon book *Bread for the World* (Paulist Press, 1975).

(3) Joseph's role in Egypt as the "Secretary of Agriculture"
    offers an interesting precedent (Gen. 39ff). What can we
    learn from this piece of biblical history?

(4) What bearing does the biblical teaching of stewardship have
    on the question of food production and distribution? (See,
    for example, Genesis 1:27 and Matthew 25:14-30.)

(5) On Sundays many Christians echo the vision of the prophet
    Isaiah when they sing: "Heaven and earth are filled with
    your glory." Can we say this to a person in Tanzania or the
    Sahel who is slowly wasting away from hunger?

(6) In the same setting, how are we to understand the words of
    Jesus (Mt. 6), "Do not be anxious, saying, 'What shall we
    eat?' or 'What shall we drink?' . . . But seek first his king-

dom and his justice, and all these things shall be yours as well"?

VI. Suggested Actions

(1) Fast (water or liquids) one day a week.
(2) Share your fast/abstinence directly with the hungry locally or through agencies reaching larger numbers.[1] (Any sharing should be from scarcity as well as from excess.)
(3) Patronize local food co-ops instead of grocery stores.
(4) Cultivate a small garden.
(5) Write letters to the president, congresspeople, church leaders, etc., regarding your willingness to reduce consumption and provide technical assistance, food aid, and food reserves to the world community.[2]
(6) Engage in public boycott of meats.
(7) Pass out leaflets at grocery stores to inform about hunger facts and suggestions.
(8) Reproduce this action list or parts of it in church bulletins or work situations.
(9) Plan liturgies for your worshiping community on the subject of hunger.
(10) Write congresspersons in favor of a separate grading system for non-grain-fed beef, so consumers can choose which beef to buy.
(11) Get and use these and other cookbooks:
     Diet for a Small Planet, Frances Moore Lappe
     Recipes for a Small Planet, Ellen Buchman Ewald
     Great Meatless Meals, by both authors (all are Ballantine Books)
(12) Order informative filmstrip (free) from Bread for the World (20 minutes with cassette) for a group education session.[3]
(13) Reduce your overall consumption of food.
(14) Waste less food.
(15) Help develop new educational programs in families,

parishes, and schools oriented toward changes in consuming patterns and personal life styles. Such programs could examine the cultural significance of eating together—stressing the fraternal values of eating together over the physical pleasures.

(16) Become an active member of Bread for the World.[4]

(17) Ask policymakers to make substantial contributions toward the creation of a world food bank (composed of wheat, rice, and coarse grains, plus fertilizers, fuels, and other agricultural resources). Current ideas include a call for regional storage depots that could be drawn upon by countries facing emergency food problems.

(18) Urge policymakers to make more concessional sales of wheat to poor nations at below market prices while subsidizing U.S. producers.

(19) Begin educating yourself to proper nutrition and meat substitutes.

(20) Personally involve yourself with local groups serving hunger.

(21) Resist advertisements and other forms of social pressure which generate affluent eating habits.

(22) Examine practices of the economic system, institutions and structures regarding wasteful and indefensible use of world resources (grain, fertilizer, meat, land).

(23) Involve groups locally in hunger program by developing organizational gardens.

(24) Use books on the study list in this chapter in conducting group study sessions.

(25) Establish (through your parish or prayer group) a food pantry for emergency hunger relief.

(26) Support increasing the purchasing power of the poor countries by paying just prices for their exports.

(27) Encourage providing more effective forms of agricultural assistance which will help developing countries to produce more food for their own peoples. Much of the assistance that is provided now does not meet the needs of the small farmer in these states.

(28) Work toward developing effective programs for the redis-

tribution of income in this country, thereby increasing the purchasing power of low-earning Americans.

(29) Support the breaking of economic and cultural patterns which downgrade agriculture and drive farming families off the land. Present practices virtually ignore fertile land which cannot be worked by large scale, "capital-intensive" machinery and methods. Emphasize the personal and social values of creative physical work and primary production (i.e., support the small farmer).

(30) Show support for increased research studies on effective stewardship of the soil and the seas, and on balanced development of the rural and urban sectors of our country.

(31) Question the goals of an economic system which urges us to consume and waste extravagantly, rather than share available food resources.

Bread for the World
Worship Aids

VIGIL

This service is recommended for use in both parish and interdenominational settings. Adaptations should be freely made to situations and needs.

The focal area should suggest the relation between food scarcity and abundance in our world. The chancel or platform area should be divided into a two-thirds area of scarcity and a one-third area of abundance. The former should contain a bare "Lectern A" and a portable "Table A" with no cloth and a few simple bowls of rice and other cereals. The one-third area should contain "Lectern B" covered with a richly decorated hanging and "Table B" covered with a rich-looking cloth and heavily laden with foods of all sorts.

A chair should be placed near each lectern. Two leaders are required, and assistants for each may be added as needed. Leader A should wear plain garments and Leader B should be richly dressed. The appearance of any assistants should correspond to the area in which they function.

A standing or hanging cross should be positioned well in back of the lecterns and tables, marking the furthermost end of the boundary between the two areas. Along the boundary from the front to rear, a wall should be constructed, using small boxes such as shoeboxes or other light materials. The wall should contain at least as many pieces as there are people in the congregation.

Other visual aids may be employed which contribute to the contrast: greenery, flowers, plants, large posters or projected slides of abundance for the one-third area, and signs of aridity and scarcity and suffering for the two-thirds area.

If the group wishes to add an additional gesture, such as the signing of a petition or a pledge for some specific action, it would be helpful to pass out the cards or forms as the people assemble.

OPENING SONG: "Morning Has Broken" (or other appropriate song)

Two leaders, with any assistants, enter and take their places.

Leader B: May the God of peace, who brought back from the dead our Lord Jesus, the great Shepherd of the sheep, by the blood of the eternal covenant, equip us fully for the doing of his will, and may he make of us what he would have us be through Jesus Christ our Lord.

All: TO CHRIST BE GLORY FOR EVER AND EVER! AMEN. (Hebrews 13:20-21)

Leader A: You cannot tell by careful watching

All: WHEN THE KINGDOM OF GOD WILL COME.

Leader A: Neither is it a matter of reporting

All: THAT IT IS "HERE" OR "THERE."

Leader A: The Kingdom of God

All: IS ALREADY IN YOUR MIDST (Luke 17:20b-21)

INTRODUCTION: In a few sentences, let one of the presiders or another leader welcome the congregation to this celebration of the Good News of Jesus Christ, in the painful context of the world's inequities and hunger, pointing out the two-thirds/one-third contrast, and inviting them to pray and participate in the actions that are to follow.

OPENING PRAYER:

Leader B: To come before God in prayer is to surrender all the pride and all the walls that now divide us. Let us gather ourselves together then in prayer.

The congregation in silent prayer.

Leader A: Almighty God our Father, whose oneness gives the lie to all that separates your children, both our affluence and our want are known to you, as is our slow desire to do your will. So let your Spirit quicken us to challenge the powers that paralyze human institutions and to change the patterns of the world's existence, that no one may countenance the continued separation of what you have joined together.

All: AMEN.

FIRST READING: Amos 8:4-7

This may be read as a dialogue, with Leader A reading verse 4, Leader B, verses 5 and 6, and Leader A, verse 7.

RESPONSE: "Whatsoever You Do to the Least of My Brothers"

SECOND READING: Luke 16:10-31

This may also be read as a dialogue, alternating between Leaders A and B as follows: A: 10-22; B: 23-24; A: 25-26; B: 27-28; A: 29; B: 30; A: 31.

THE MESSAGE: Depending on the occasion, the size of the congregation, and the circumstances, this section could take one of a number of forms: (1) a dialogue between Leaders A and B, with B approaching the readings and the message of Jesus from the point of view of the comfortable who are sincerely trying to understand the Good News of Jesus and A from the point of view of the suffering; (2) a dialogue between the leaders and the congregation, with initial statements from the leaders about how the current food problem looks, first to affluent eyes and then to the eyes of the undernourished, inviting questions and reflections from the congregation; or (3) as a traditional sermon. The following thoughts are offered as optional guideposts for any of these.

REFLECTION:

In his play, "The Lady's Not for Burning," Christopher Fry has one of his characters say: "All one can do is make wherever one is as much like home as possible." For the prophets and for Jesus, "home" is the Kingdom of God, where love and justice and peace prevail. And they are always calling us to make wherever we are as much like home as possible.

Most of us do just the opposite: we make ourselves at home wherever we are. Like the rich man "who dressed in purple linen and feasted splendidly every day," we accept our affluent situation and usually manage to check any impulse to make it a little more like the Kingdom, a little more like home.

"Home" for the prophets is neither of these two areas we

see before us: the one-third area of affluence and abundance, nor the two-thirds area of scarcity and want. They refuse to accept either as "home." Thus, they shake us up, make us uncomfortable with our easy adjustment to such a world, and we resist letting them get through to us.

No prophet ever got through to that rich man in the gospel story. Jesus tells us that he lived his whole life just making himself at home wherever he was. It never occurred to him how far from "home" he really was, dining splendidly every day, while a beggar lay dying at his gate. Not until he himself experienced suffering did the dawn break, and then it was too late.

Amos says *now* is the time for justice. Jesus says *now* is the day of salvation. *Now* is the time to begin making wherever we are as much like home as possible. We cannot accept either of these isolated ghettos that we see symbolized before us, nor can we accept a world divided into two-thirds hungry and one-third over-fed. Neither alone nor both together is fit to be called "home" by the sons and daughters of God. Home happens when the cross breaks down the wall between them, redeems them, and makes them one in Christ. And the beginning of the way home lies in sharing.

Here may follow any pledges or commitments the people are invited to make. Cards or forms may be deposited in a basket or offering plate as the people come forward for the COMMISSIONING OF ONE ANOTHER.

The two lecterns are now moved in front of the "wall" and at the boundary between the two areas. The two leaders may take different parts of the following prayer, or one person may lead it.

PRAYER OF BLESSING:

Leader: The Lord be with you.
All: AND ALSO WITH YOU.
Leader: Lift up your hearts.
All: WE LIFT THEM UP TO THE LORD.
Leader: Let us give thanks to the Lord our God.

All: IT IS RIGHT TO GIVE HIM THANKS AND
          PRAISE.

Leader: We give you thanks, we praise and bless you,
          Almighty, ever-living God;
          we praise you for all your deeds,
          for your patient revelation,
          for your Spirit's moving us and leading us reluctant
          people
          toward the freedom and the unity
          that the enslaved and the divided find in you.
          We praise you most for Jesus, your Word in our own
          flesh,
          who touches us with his hands and makes us whole,
          who stretched out his hand to the leper, touched him,
          and said, "I do will it. Be cured." (Matthew 8:3)
          Who, finding Peter's mother-in-law ill,
          "took her by the hand and the fever left her." (Mat-
          thew 8:15)
          Who, in answer to those who asserted death's domin-
          ion,
          "entered and took her by the hand, and the little girl
          got up." (Matthew 9:25)
          We give thanks for hands and for our sense of touch.
          Touch our hands, that our touch may then bring
          strength, may accept and reconcile, soothe and com-
          fort, reach out to give and share, to offer courage and
          support and oneness to your people. Open these hands
          of ours, extend these arms of ours,
          to give as well as to seek forgiveness,
          to heal as well as to be healed.
          And let our hands reject all grasping and all greed,
          all willful force and violence,
          and be in Jesus' name a sign of care.
          Through Christ our Lord.
          Amen.

All: AMEN.

This portion of the service should be explained either in a writ-
ten program or orally. The leaders move in front of the lecterns.

If the assembly is large, others may assist them, and should join them at the front.

During the singing of an appropriate song ("Let the Spirit in," "One Man's [Person's, Christian's] Hands," or other selection), let the people come forward, leaving any pledge or commitment cards in the appointed container, and stand before one of the leaders. Each leader then places his/her hands on the shoulders of the person immediately before him/her, holding the hands there for a moment in silence.

THE COMMISSIONING OF ONE ANOTHER: Then let the reader speak these words from 1 John 3:18: "Brother (sister), let us love not in word alone, but in deed and truth." Then the leader withdraws his/her hands from the shoulders of the person before him/her, goes to the "wall," removes one of the pieces, places it at the foot of the cross, and is seated.

The person who was commissioned then takes the place of the leader, and so commissions the person in front of him/her, placing hands on the shoulders for a silent moment, repeating the words from 1 John 3:18, and, in turn, taking a piece of the wall to the foot of the cross, and returning to his/her seat.

This action is repeated until everyone present has been commissioned, ministered the commission, removed a portion of the wall, and placed it at the foot of the cross, and returned to his/her seat.

Any boxes or pieces of the wall remaining after all are seated should be removed by the leaders and taken to the foot of the cross. Then the two portable tables should be brought together, and foods distributed evenly and equally over their surfaces.

When all are in their places again, let there be a few moments of silence. Then a leader gestures for the people to stand.

DISMISSAL:

Leader: May Almighty God grant us the grace to persevere in all that we have undertaken, that we may be good and faithful stewards over the trust that he has given us, even unto the end. Through Christ our Lord. Amen.

All: AMEN. MARANATHA. COME, LORD JESUS.

It may be deemed appropriate in some situations to reverse the order of the closing song and the dismissal.

CLOSING SONG: "A Charge To Keep I Have," "In Christ

There Is No East or West" or other appropriate song.

PRAYER SERVICE

This service is appropriate for informal situations and is particularly suitable for small groups. It may serve equally well for parish or interdenominational use.

The people are seated in a circle or concentric circles with a table in the center supporting a large open Bible and a copy of a daily newspaper, placed so they face and confront each other. In large assemblies where the circle arrangement is not possible, portable lecterns, one holding the open Bible, the other holding the newspaper, may be placed front center fairly close to each other, partly facing the congregation and partly facing each other.

A person or persons assigned in advance to excerpt stories and comments about world hunger from newspapers of the preceding week or weeks should be prepared to read one or two sentences from each during the service. Another person or persons should be prepared to read previously selected Scripture quotations related to hunger, justice, sharing, or stewardship in general. Before the service, the newspaper excerpts and the Scripture quotations should be matched as appropriately as possible, so that in the DIALOGUE section of the service, the biblical passages proclaim the word and the news excerpts indicate our response. Between five and ten "sets" should be prepared.

OPENING SONG: "Simple Gifts"

GREETING (Leader)
May the simplicity and love of a child of God be yours.

INTRODUCTION (Another Leader):
Sisters and brothers, we are here to praise God and to find strength and courage for the struggle. Because we believe, we choose to struggle. The Word of God judges and challenges our times, our lives, and our institutions. The Word of God contradicts many of our established ways, and calls us to a higher obedience. Hence the struggle. And it is a struggle in which the stakes are high.

In an editorial in the *Washington Post* (7/17/74), Colman McCarthy wrote: "History has never seen a country collectively decide to sacrifice its standard of living for the goal of relieving the suffering of another country. If anything, as in war, it is always the opposite—citizens will sacrifice for the purpose of increasing the misery of the other tribe. So, in this sense, there is a war on, with people dying of hunger as painfully as though bombs or napalm fell on them. And this war appears to have few protesters in America, only a congressional committee or two, and a few people who see a moral link between their own plentiful food supply and the non-supply of the hungry."

This is indeed a hard saying. We may not agree with every word, but it clearly points to the struggle. And it is this struggle we pray about today (tonight).

PRAYER (Leader):
Your Word, O God, is mighty to create
and is life-giving for all those who hear.
Touch with your Spirit our attentions, minds and hearts,
and make us ready for your Word.
Help us to find in Scripture
the message of your saving love writ large and spoken loud
for feeble eyes and ears like ours,
to cleanse us and awaken our trust in you
to make us bold for the struggle.
Through Christ our Lord. Amen.

FIRST READING: Isaiah 32:1-8

RESPONSE: "Let There Be Peace on Earth" (or other appropriate song)

SECOND READING: John 1:1-5, 10-14.

SILENT PRAYER
The group may pray in silence, or people may be invited, as they choose, to offer individual prayers aloud. After the silence is well established, or when people have had sufficient opportunity for spontaneous prayer, the dialogue may begin.

DIALOGUE BETWEEN WORD AND WORLD

The Bible passages and the corresponding press excerpts are here read alternately by different persons, in the following order: Bible passages, second press excerpt, more silence, and so on, through the five or ten brief "sets."

SONG: "I Cannot Come to the Banquet"

Or other appropriate song. The use of the recording of the song following the Scripture reading in Bernstein's Mass may also be deemed appropriate in place of a congregational song.

DISCUSSION

In small assemblies, the discussion can be general, involving all in an effort to apply the Word of God to the world hunger scene, problems of production and distribution of food, the kind of life-style such a climate seems to demand, types of governmental action that are called for, and so on.

In large groups, perhaps three or four people could be prepared to present suggested courses of action: on the individual or household level, on the parish or local church level, on the U.S. government level, and on the level of world planning and cooperation.

In either case, the goal should be to reach some consensus on a course or courses of action to which the group may wish to bind itself in covenant with one another and with God. Let the discussion conclude with at least some consensus resolution for action on one or more of the above levels, and some determination of ways for carrying out those commitments.

BLESSING (Leader):
With this in mind, we pray always that our God may count us worthy of his calling, and mightily bring to fulfillment every good purpose and every act inspired by faith, so that the name of our Lord Jesus may be glorified in us, and we in him, according to the grace of our God and the Lord Jesus Christ. Amen. (From 2 Thessalonians 1:11-12)

CLOSING SONG: "This Is Our Accepted Time" (or other appropriate song).

It may be deemed appropriate in some situations to reverse the order of the closing song and the blessing or benediction.

7
MEDIA

by

James W. Fahey

For our modern problem is not the firm control of mass media, but the creative and constructive development of its content. Our aim should not be to force mass media into a particular system but to release it from its own bonds and set it free.

Stanley I. Stuber

I. Introduction

Media include newspapers, magazines, books, telephone, telegraph, radio, television, etc. In fact, a medium can be any delivery system which outputs information that can be received into the human information processing system via sight, sound, touch, taste, or smell.

For the purposes of the discussion here the main focus will be on the medium of television. Why concentrate on television? Television is the current revolution in communications. Coaxial cable, satellite, laser, and fiber optics are developments in delivery systems, but these systems all have the sending of video and/or audio signals in common. In short, they have television as their main commodity.

Commercial television is currently the most pervasive communication medium of our time. Today it is mostly on an output basis. There is little chance for television programming to be interchanged between consumer and signal origination. Digital computing and cable technology may change all that. When the coaxial cable reaches the same saturation point that over the air broadcasting now enjoys, there will be more of an opportunity for the consumer to control his own programming choices and to feed information back into the system.

Another reason for focusing on television here results from its enormous teaching potential. We have had a generation of individuals who have grown up with television. These are people who never knew an environment without television. Today man's environment is almost total communication. In the morning man is awakened by his clock radio. While he gets ready for work he listens to and sometimes watches the news. If he drives to work he listens to the car radio and reads the billboard signs as he drives along the highway. If someone else does the driving (car pool, rapid transit, bus, train, etc.) he reads the morning newspaper. And so it goes all day long until his clock radio lulls him to sleep at night. Man is exposed today to communication stimuli which he perceives constantly and which he must share concurrently with all other members of society.

Television is not only pervasive, it is also prolific. Some areas of the country have continuous programming. Television is a video as well as an audio medium. The consumer uses it in the privacy of his own home, but the messages he receives are very much intended as public communications. There is a cultural leavening that television accomplishes that no other medium has come close to offering.

It is for these reasons that we chose to single out television. Let us look at some issues.

Admittedly, violence is not the only issue that consumers of the media should be concerned about, but it provides an excellent starting point for our discussion. The sixth volume of the Surgeon General's report on the effects of televised violence is the summary volume. It outlines and summarizes the studies presented in five other volumes. The rhubarb over the summary volume is that it equivocates and qualifies regarding the statement it makes concerning the effects of watching televised violence and the increase of aggressive behavior on the part of the young. What follows is an example of such equivocation; try it on for size.

> Thus, there is a convergence of fairly substantial experimental evidence for short run causation of aggression among some children by viewing violence on the screen and the much less certain evidence from field studies that extensive violence viewing precedes some long run manifestations of aggressive behavior. This convergence of the two types of evidence constitutes some preliminary indication of a causal relationship, but a good deal of research remains to be done before one can have confidence in these conclusions.[1]

Wait a minute. What do you mean by convergence? Isn't there one study that answers the question with a flat yes or no? Does the question still remain "Is there a causal relationship between viewing violence and subsequent violent behavior acted out by the viewer'"? Senator Pastore called the Surgeon General's report a "scientific and cultural breakthrough." Paraphrasing the report he said:

> For we now know there is a causal relation between televised violence and antisocial behavior which is sufficient to warrant immediate remedial action.[2]

Eli Rubenstein who was the editor of that multi-volume report said that perhaps Senator Pastore's remarks about a scientific and cultural breakthrough were more than a little generous.[3] On the other hand the scientists conducting the studies that were summarized in the sixth volume, the members of the Senate Subcommittee on Communication, and witnesses called before that committee agreed that there was, in Pastore's words, evidence sufficient to warrant immediate remedial action. After the report was published in 1972 and the subcommittee was still holding hearings on the matter, television network officials called before the committee to testify acknowledged the report and agreed that some television programming might indeed be a negative influence on the behavior of children.[4]

Subsequently Liebert and his associates have tallied up 146 published papers which represent fifty studies of over 10,000 youthful subjects from every variety of background.[5] These studies *all* indicate that violence viewing increases aggressive behavior on the part of youthful viewers. Certainly based on this information, what Senator Pastore has said is not only cogent, but it is increasingly urgent as well. Immediate remedial action was called for then; it is still called for today.

The American Medical Association on July 2, 1976 passed a resolution urging its members to activate opposition to excessive television violence. The AMA resolution calls television violence an environmental hazard that threatens the health and welfare of young Americans. The AMA intends to produce a booklet explaining the effects of televised violence and brutality. The book will be handed out in doctors' offices and distributed directly from doctor to patient.[6]

Doesn't it stand to reason though that something is happening to our children as a result of viewing television? We send our children off to school at about the age of five. By the time they get through high school at eighteen they have had approximately 13,000 contact hours with their teachers in their classrooms. Our hope is that they've learned something. We give them graduation certificates to verify the time spent in the classroom and the successful completion of a course of study. Peggy Charren of Action for Children's Television (ACT) tells us that by the time a youngster finishes high school he has spent some 15,000 hours in front of the television set.[7] It makes one wonder what kind of learning has taken place as a result of 15,000 contact hours with a television set. Dr. Harry J. Skornia has made the point that television itself is neutral,[8] but that the programming a person is exposed to teaches him about himself, others, and his environment just as classroom instruction teaches him about these things. What he is taught in either case can be good or bad.

We would rid our classrooms, in the wink of an eye, of a teacher who raped, robbed, pillaged, cheated, plundered, gored, and murdered in full view of his students (undoubtedly covert actions like these would result in dismissal too), and yet we often allow our children to be babysat by programming that acts out the same violent behaviors in front of them. What kinds of pictures of reality develop in these children's minds?

Lyle tells us that for all age groups about one-quarter of the children watch television more than five hours a day on schooldays.[9] For these children, then, for every classroom contact hour there is also a television contact hour. When weekend viewing habits are included, it is easy to see how the toll mounts to 15,000 contact hours between television and child. Ms. Charren's claim is not at all unrealistic.

Network efforts at establishing a family viewing hour aren't much help for after school hours or for Saturday morning programming. Family viewing of non-violent programming was scheduled during the first evening hour of prime time. It is now under fire from both the industry and from media consumers. After school viewing hours often consist of programming too violent to be shown during family viewing time. How does this happen? These shows may be in the form of syndicated reruns or movies whose content is not checked by local stations since there are no restrictions for violence during that viewing time period.

But we shouldn't think that only children are adversely affected by programming on television. George Gerbner and Larry Gross have pointed out that Americans watching prime time television more than four hours a day think the world is more dangerous than those who watch two hours a day or less think it is.[10] The more you watch the worse your picture of reality becomes. Gerbner and Gross have gone beyond the question of violence viewing and subsequent violent behavior. What they are saying is that television is a very strong means of social control. Television is teaching the power of authority—who does what and gets away with it, who doesn't get away with it and why, and what role does a victim play. It is also teaching us the acceptance of violence as a social behavior. We no longer abhor violence in real life situations, unless, of course, they happen to us. Heavy television viewers are less trustful of their fellow citizens. They fear the real world more than light viewers do. For heavy viewers the world is a dangerous and frightening place. Prime time television programming may be helping to create real world paranoids. Heavy viewers were more likely to predict higher incidents of actual personal involvement in some type of violence during any given week than were light viewers.[11]

U.C.L.A. psychiatrists Roderic Gorney and David Loye recently reported findings of their study of 260 couples. They found that the viewing of violent television increased the occurrence of "unhelpful" behavior and caused an alarming difference in values. Dr. Loye pointed to the fact that while the measurement of behavioral differences is important, the measurement of the change in values in adults is the more important finding.[12]

Perhaps we need to flip the coin though, and we should make an effort to appreciate and pay attention to what good things television has to offer to us. We need to magnify them, emphasize them, and figure out a way of making money through them—more money than is made through the programming that is abhorrent to us. Thus we will change the programming picture rapidly. Until that great discovery is made, however, we will have to content ourselves with questions of a more immediately practical nature. How can we as consumers help to make the system better right now? What kinds of responsibilities for public affairs programming are incumbent upon license holders who are using the natural resources of the public airwaves? Licenses are granted to broadcasters by the Federal Communications Commission (F.C.C.). Broadcasters' technical facilities must meet certain specification standards and they must broadcast in the spectrum space and at the power assigned to them. Further they are required to broadcast for the public interest, convenience, and necessity.

Important policy questions that concern us all—media users, creators, consumers, processors, and deliverers of information—are paramount to the development of a communications system that truly serves the public interest, convenience, and necessity. We must begin to structure our communication goals as a nation. Everyone must be involved, for no one is isolated from the problems. We do not want to wind up serving a communication system that should have been designed to be of service to us.

The social effects of the media; media interfaces within education with students, faculty, parents, administrators, and staff; industrial and organizational communication systems and needs; governmental questions of foreign and domestic communications; communication needs of the average citizen; welfare questions; cable hook-ups to limited income families; communication needs of the aged; system designs with time and planning for phase-in and phase-out—these are but a few of the basic problem areas we are facing immediately.

Broadcasters, parents, teachers, students, housepersons, business executives, and governmental officials need not only be concerned about the violence issue; they need also be concerned about working together to develop the maximum service potential of our American communication system.

II. Study Bibliography

Johnson, Nicholas. *How To Talk Back to Your Television Set.* Little, Brown and Co.: Boston, 1970.

Liebert, R. M., Neale, J. M., and Davidson, E. S. *The Early Window: Effects of Television on Children and Youth.* Pergamon Press: Elmsford, New York, 1973.

Methvin, Eugene H. "What You Can Do About TV Violence." *Reader's Digest*, July 1975.

Shayon, Robert Lewis. *The Crowd-Catchers: Introducing Television.* Saturday Review Press: New York, 1973.

III. Reflections as a Christian

If the Church (i.e., Christianity) wants to be relevant to modern man, and that is its mission, then the Church must learn to communicate with modern man. That is certainly not a new idea, nor is it really revolutionary. It could have been said in the heyday of any society in any age.

Throughout history the Church has trained scholars and leaders in traditional disciplines as well as in newer modes. The Church has trained excellent doctors, lawyers, psychologists, sociologists, teachers, preachers, prophets, and healers of all varieties. Today it is more urgent than ever before that the Church understand the mores and the culture of the times and of the people. It is urgent that the Church (who is the Church? —don't look at your brother, look at yourself—you are the Church) understand human communication and modern communication systems.

Today it is not enough to take a passing interest in press, cinema, radio, television, newspapers, and magazines. We must be vitally concerned with the powers that program these media. Advertising, marketing, public relations, propaganda, persuasion, group dynamics, and intercultural communications are all very necessary to the existence of the Christian in the modern world. This list is by no means exhaustive; every aspect of human communication needs to be scrutinized, learned, and utilized by the Church in modern society.

Walt Kelly's Pogo has said "We has met the enemy, and they is us!" We need to stop being our own worst enemy. Communication is not a one-way street. It is not all take, nor is it all give. We must do our share of taking, or receiving, messages, but we must also do our share of giving, or sending messages to a world sorely in need of the message of salvation brought by Jesus Christ.

The Church needs trained and active communicologists who are indeed aware of the technological advances made in the area of mass communication especially. These communicologists need to dedicate their talents to making the Kingdom of God a reality. We need to experience the concrete reality and presence of salvation in our time and in our day. We cannot leave the work for another generation. It must be done now.

We need to arouse in the hearts of mankind a hunger and a thirst for social justice. We need to help all men establish within themselves a craving for fraternal charity in all of their actions and in the truth and reality of their lives. We need to help all men elevate themselves above conditions of poverty and misery. Christians must be instrumental in the raising of all men to a level of human dignity befitting them and befitting the return in glory of Jesus Christ.

Modern communication methods are certainly no quick and easy guarantee that all of these things will be accomplished. But what is certain is that modern man cannot be reached except through modern communication channels and messages.

Scripture Passages for Reflection

John 1:12-14
Luke 12:15-31
2 Timothy 2:2
2 Timothy 3:2-9

IV. Questions for Reflection/Discussion

(1) Part of a station's license agreement is to serve public interest, convenience, and necessity. What does this mean? What should it mean?

(2) What is meant by the term "public airwaves"?

(3) What is the public's responsibility for the airwaves? What is the broadcaster's responsibility?

(4) What should the Christian attitude be toward give-away gimmickry?

(5) What constitutes exploitative programming?

(6) What constitutes exploitative advertising?

V. Suggested Actions

(1) Develop a guide for effective viewing and distribute it at your parish, your P.T.A. meeting, etc. (There are effective guides for reading—why not for viewing?)

(2) Watch television with the children.

(3) Limit the number of hours per day you will allow the set to be on.

(4) Select (with your child) the programming. (Make up your mind at the beginning of the week.)

(5) Enjoy other activities regularly with your children—reading, museums, art shows, etc.

(6) Monitor the programs you watch, i.e., when you or your child sees something annoying, try to mark down the time of the program, the network, and the sponsor. This works equally well when you see something you like, too.

(7) Follow up #6 with letters or postcards of protest or praise from you, your group, or your media organization. (See Action Address List for network addresses.)

(8) Watch programs that stimulate children to some productive activity after the show is over (hobby and craft shows, shows with outdoor activities, etc.)

(9) Support public television.

(10) Write Action for Children's Television for information about its work. (P.O. Box 510, Boston, Massachusetts 02102)

(11) Write the National Association of Broadcasters (485 Madison Avenue, New York City, 10020) for information about its work.

(12) Write the National Association for Better Broadcasting (P.O. Box 43640, Los Angeles, California, 90043) to find out how you can support its work.

(13) After gathering information, design an exhibit on media information for bank lobbies, school libraries, train stations, etc.

(14) Using the books and article in the study bibliography as well as other sources, develop a media bibliography for your local school or public library. Raise funds to supply these books for the library.

(15) Sign up for training programs that teach citizens how to use newer communication technologies.

(16) Follow communication legislation and express your views to those who vote.

(17) Check local educational institutions to see if they have media education or other communications programs. Support establishment of such programs.

(18) When your local station's license to operate comes up for review (it does so at regular intervals), write the Federal Communications Commission (see Action Address List) with your views on the station's performance.

(19) Develop methods for educating parents and children on how to watch television (newsletters, seminars, weekly program suggestion guides, etc.).

(20) Increase your media literacy every day by learning something new about communication technology, its application and its possible effects.

8

MENTAL ILLNESS

A thirteen-year-old girl, identified as Carla and described as "borderline retarded," was sent involuntarily to the Brookwood Center for Girls in Claverack, New York (in 1971). There, her "treatment" consisted of solitary confinement for three consecutive days on three occasions and four days on another.

Robert A. Liston
Patients or Prisoners:
The Mentally Ill in America

I. Introduction

What is mental health? Mental health has to do with the human being functioning as an emotionally mature individual. Emotional maturity is difficult to get a handle on because it is abstract in nature and is always in flux. We are always in the process of growth to emotional maturity. Like happiness, it is not a place but a direction.

Approximately one in every ten persons in this country is not mentally healthy.[1] How do we define this condition? "In simplest terms, mental illness is a disorder, disease, or disturbance that keeps a person from living as happily and healthily as he—and perhaps others—would like. Considered more technically, it is a complex of brain disorders."[2] If a *pattern* of emotionally immature behavior exists, this could characterize mental illness.

These groupings summarize the major kinds of mental illness: psychoses, neuroses, personality disorders, psychosomatic illnesses, and organic brain disorders. Each of these is not exclusive necessarily of the others.[3]

Is mental illness fatal? Not in itself, no, but many suicides result from mental disorders, especially depression. Out of 200,000 known suicide attempts each year, approximately 25,000 people manage to take their own lives. Suicide is in the top ten causes of death.[4] It is important to note that these figures do not include the plethora of unreported suicide attempts that occur each year.

How do we care for those of our mentally ill who do not commit suicide? The following description is an example of what we have been providing for the mentally ill in state hospital facilities. Ten years ago I visited a state hospital near my college. It was like every foul description I had read about such institutions. We walked through puddles of urine on stairways into dirty, drab, cavernous rooms lined with people sitting in uncomfortable straight-backed chairs. These rooms housed the least ill. In another building we entered yet another large, drab room which held the catatonic and more seriously ill patients. I recall one had taken a position curled up in a squat against a sizzling hot radiator. The patients' clothes were virtually in rags and did not fit. They had obviously not been washed for days, and received less care than animals at an underfunded city zoo. If this was treatment, I thought, what must hell be like?

Although the trend is toward community mental health care, state hospitals and similar facilities do exist today and must be upgraded while we are working toward getting most of the patient population into smaller facilities or into out-patient care. One author suggests that the state hospitals which serve a relatively small region might be turned into regional mental health centers.

The state hospitals are to a large extent existing to serve the "out of sight, out of mind" attitude that the larger population chooses to hold toward the mentally ill. In the large proportion of such institutions patients are literally locked away. One doctor states, "The state hospital must not become a dumping ground for those patients of community mental health centers whose treatment seems not particularly rewarding. Depending on local conditions and prejudices, patients at risk of being dumped into the state hospital system are members of minority groups, the poor, the mentally retarded, alcoholics and other addicts, the aged, some adolescents, and the uneducated."[5]

What principles should guide us in our search to improve the conditions and treatment of patients in such institutions? In a recent issue of *MH* (Mental Hygiene) magazine, T. M. Madison enumerated these patients' rights:

(1) the right to be treated with basic dignity and respect;
(2) the right to decide what is going to happen and why, including the right to consent to or refuse any treatment;
(3) the right to physical privacy and confidentiality of information;
(4) the right to the *whole truth*, including access to medical records.

Undergirding these rights should be a solid relationship between the patients and the providers of health care.[6]

It is vital that within the state hospital system the following principles should be adhered to:

(1) fostering of the independence of patients;
(2) introducing of democratic principles in the hospital care system to replace the present widespread attitude of paternalism;
(3) converting of the closed society of the hospital into an open one;
(4) freeing the dormant human potentials of both patients and staff.[7]

Within the last ten years we have made strides in reorienting in terms of our mental health care. Just prior to his death in 1963, President John F. Kennedy signed into law a bill which set up and would eventually help to finance Community Mental Health Centers. There are now five hundred such centers in this country, reinforcing the trend toward community mental health care.

In addition, the National Association of Mental Health reports other gains. Fifty-one percent of our population now has some insurance coverage for mental illness. The principle of "right to treatment" is winning in the courts. Employment barriers are dropping. The U.S. Civil Service, for example, has dropped its discriminatory pre-employment question about nervous breakdown. Since any changes in conditions will be and must be preceded by attitude change, it was gratifying to note that although Senator Thomas Eagleton was dropped from the 1972 national Democratic ticket, he was re-elected to the United States Senate from his home state of Missouri.[8]

Although we have spent much of our discussion to this point on the institutionalized mentally ill, in fact the vast majority of patient care at present is not institutional care, but rather it is out-patient care. At present, eighty percent of all care for the mentally ill in this country is now on an out-patient basis. Partly because of the introduction of drug therapy in the late 1950's and partly because of the phasing out of hospitals in several states, the number of patients discharged annually has risen from 126,000 in 1955 to 419,000 in 1972.[9]

Many patients, however, are now being released because of administrative reasons rather than therapeutic reasons. Currently, one-third of the 419,000 released patients (or 130,000) have no place to go upon release and are not capable of fending for themselves. They need support upon being released. They need someone or some group to provide them with decent meals and assist them in taking their medication. Halfway houses are one very important answer for these persons.

The National Association of Mental Health is presently aware of only 209 halfway houses in the entire country. In all of New Jersey there is only one halfway house. New York State has eleven such places but all of New York's put together serve only 388 persons. As one result of this deficiency, the death rate among discharged patients is five to ten percent higher in some areas then it is among patients who remain in the state hospitals.[10]

In view of the foregoing facts, is there a formula for reducing the mental illness problem in the United States? Robert Liston, in his startling book *Patients or Prisoners: The Mentally Ill in America*, offers these guidelines:

(1) House the patients in small facilities where they will receive human care and as much therapy as possible.
(2) Disperse these facilities throughout the community so that the patients can be part of the community and make use of its services, such as libraries, theaters, museums, schools, hospitals, and places of employment.
(3) Keep as many patients as possible at home, assisting them and their families as much as possible through out-patient care at clinics and through visits from social workers.
(4) Provide enough trained personnel so that every patient receives regular medical care and various forms of psychotherapy and counseling.[11]

Underlying the approaches to treatment both within institutions and in out-patient care should be the principle of fostering the independence of the mentally ill. This is another way of saying that we should be committed to solid treatment (at the community level) because independence goes hand in hand with mental health.

II. Study Bibliography

Liston, Robert A. *Patients or Prisoners: The Mentally Ill in America.* Franklin Watts: New York, 1976.

MH (Mental Hygiene) magazine. You can keep abreast of some of the latest developments in the field of mental health by reading this regularly. Most libraries have subscriptions.

Harris, Thomas A., M.D. *I'm OK—You're OK.* Harper and Row: New York, 1969.

IV. Reflections as a Christian

We can safely say that Jesus Christ is in favor of each human person being allowed to grow to his full potentialities. Mental illness is an enormous hurdle that inhibits this growth.

The mentally ill have a "right to treatment." Putting them in institutions and feeding them and giving them tranquilizers does not qualify as treatment. This is not the Christian approach to fostering independence and health for every person. The "freedom to be sick, helpless and isolated," says Robert Liston, "is not freedom."

By shutting away or ignoring the mentally ill in our communities we are validating the thoroughly American and thoroughly anti-Christian theory that one is valuable only in proportion to how "useful" one is. And in our society "usefulness" is most often defined as contributing to the growth of the gross national product. Being able to do a full day's work for a full day's pay is the litmus test of a person's "usefulness."

It makes us uncomfortable to acknowledge the presence of those who cannot "contribute" to society in the ways and to the degrees which we think are important. We cannot deprive the mentally ill of their liberty, however, just because we do not like to acknowledge their presence. Especially for the institutionalized mentally ill, we must not only acknowledge their presence but also become their spokespersons. The mentally ill have no lobby. For these institutionalized, separate is not equal. We must seek them out and love them. Our active concern will involve determining who they are and helping to work out solid programs to love them better, and to assist them on the road to mental health. Not to accord patients the rights discussed in the introductory section of this chapter is to hamstring them in their efforts to heal.

In a way we would be ministering to the mentally ill because of selfish reasons. If any part of the body of humankind is hurting, the whole body suffers. When we help to heal the mentally ill we are making a real contribution to the whole human enterprise on this earth, and to the health of the body which is the church.

The institutionalized mentally ill are last on this earth. One would assume that they will be first in the Kingdom. But the Kingdom has been established. It is an "already" as well as a "not yet." It would seem the fulfillment of God's promise to the mentally ill should begin here and now. Let it begin with us Christians.

Scripture Passages for Reflection

Psalm 34:17-19
Galatians 6:2
1 John 4:19-21
1 Corinthians 12:24-26

IV. Questions for Reflection/Discussion

(1) Do you have adequate mental health services in your community?
(2) What would the value be in your visiting a state or private mental hospital in your area?
(3) "Like drug addicts, the mentally ill have a right to treatment." Do you agree or disagree? Discuss.
(4) What, if anything, do the mentally ill contribute to our society?

(5) Viktor Frankl has said, "An incurably psychotic individual may lose his usefulness but yet retain the dignity of a human being." As a group make a list of five things necessary to your own human dignity.

(6) As a group decide on and take one specific action to help bring each of the five requisites for human dignity to patients of a mental health institution in your area.

V. Suggested Actions

(1) With your group read Robert Liston's *Patients or Prisoners*. Discuss together its implications.

(2) Make an outline of Robert Liston's four-point formula for success in mental health care. Then check out mental institutions in your area to see how they stack up in regard to each point.

(3) Contact the volunteer coordinator of a mental health institution in your community and ask in what ways your group can contribute services.

(4) Write the National Association of Mental Health, 1800 N. Kent St., Arlington, Va. 22209, for information about how your group can help in mental health at the community and national levels.

(5) Write the National Association of Mental Health (see #4) for a list of print-outs (many are free) on a variety of topics (e.g., "Mental Health and the Law," "Pastoral Counseling," "Civil Rights of Mental Patients") as well as for a free film catalogue, and other service publications.

(6) Use the materials you receive for individual and group study as well as to plan seminars, exhibitions, film studies, and so forth, on mental health/mental illness.

(7) Call for a moratorium on administrative discharges. Before patients in your community and state mental health institutions are discharged it should be clear that they have a place to go.

(8) Write the National Association for Retarded Children to

ask what you can do to assist them in their work: 2709 Avenue E East, Arlington, Texas 76010.

(9) Associate yourself with a consumer group (or start a consumer group) in your community and initiate a patient advocate position for a mental health institution in your community or region.[1]

(10) Support increasing citizen participation in mental health program planning and in the operations of the remaining state hospitals.

The following suggested actions are adapted from a list in the book *Mental Health/Mental Illness*.[2]

(11) Support research to uncover knowledge about mental health and mental illness.

(12) Redouble efforts to increase and maintain in adequate numbers the kind of mental health workers needed in all areas.

(13) With 500 community mental health centers at present, work for the number to be increased to 1,500 by 1980. Write your congresspersons to this effect.

(14) Support expansion of public and private health insurance to provide better protection for more people.

(15) Support improvement and expansion of such mental health services for children and youth as health examinations, counseling, and treatment. (How many counselors does your children's school have—in addition to vocational counselors?)

(16) Encourage development of a sane family planning and population control service to dampen the population explosion.

(17) Assist in providing facilities and treatment services for alcoholics, drug addicts and delinquents in cooperation with community mental health centers and other resources throughout the country.

(18) Continue efforts to improve state laws related to the treatment of the mentally ill.

(19) Similarly strive to improve the nation's mental hospitals

and make them places of care and effective treatment rather than dumping grounds.

(20) Protect and promote mental health as well as prevent and reduce mental illness through improved housing, strengthened education, better and more effective welfare aid, job training, and other environmental programs.

9
POVERTY

Can there be life before death?

*On the wall of a
Belfast slum*

I. Introduction

To be poor is to be without adequate housing, food, medical care, and clothing. It is to be economically dependent or unproductive. It is to be powerless. Its roots grow out of a combination of economic and social factors.

I recall my brother's social worker friend who worked in the St. Louis slums in 1970. He recounted to my brother a number of stories of people who made up his caseload. One elderly destitute woman was so ill and obese that she could not get out of her chair or move without assistance. When the rats came she could not fend them off and they ate a number of her toes. We related this particular story to a friend of ours who had an important job with the Department of Housing and Urban Development. He calmly said, "It isn't so. There just aren't any people that poor in our country who couldn't get medical and other forms of help in situations like that. Stories about rats are exaggerated." We then told him of a group of welfare mothers in a St. Louis housing project who banded together to fight the rats. Each night they would bring their children together to sleep in the same room. One mother would stay awake all night and beat the rats away from the children with a broom. They took (and for all I know are still taking) turns in this labor of love.

There are approximately twenty-six million poor, the government tells us.[1] The government standards, many say, are not reasonable. If we include in our estimates the near poor families, that is, those who are so close to the line that any disaster or emergency or layoff would mean instant poverty, then the figure would be more like thirty-six million poor, or one in every six persons.[2] This figure is still conservative in the opinion of many.

We are not a society of equals. The Declaration of Independence guarantees not equality but equality of opportunity, not happiness but the pursuit of it. Ask a welfare mother of six who cannot find decent day care so that she can work, and can't find work so that she can pay for decent day care if she feels she has opportunities equal to that of other Americans. The bicentennial celebrations of the tenets of the Declaration of Independence were an insult to this woman.

Myths abound regarding the poor: "Oh, they're so happy the way they are." I call that the "one big happy tenement myth." If people outside the poor neighborhoods think things are so jolly there, why are they fleeing to the suburbs in record numbers?

Another myth is that all that welfare money is going to able-bodied workers who are just lazy. Seventy-five percent of all poor people are *not capable of working*! Of the twenty-five percent who are capable, 23.6 percent do work full- or part-time. Ninety-five percent of all poor who are capable of work do work.[3]

Seventy-five percent of the poor people are not capable of working? "Come on," the myth purveyors say. "Most of them are just moochers who say they're not capable of holding down a job." According to the *World Almanac* these are the "moochers" who receive welfare: the elderly, those who receive aid for dependent children (families in need because of a parent's death, continued disability or absence), the blind, the permanently and totally disabled.[4]

Who are the poor? The largest segment of the poor is non-Spanish speaking poor whites (sixty percent), but only ten percent of the total white population is poor. One-third of all blacks are poor. Forty to fifty percent of all native Americans are poor (besides taking their land, we have kept them poor). Four out of ten poor persons are children.[5]

The poor are not easy to spot because of the availability of second-hand clothes and because they frequently do not have distended bellies in our own country. Many are not underweight. The cheapest foods are those that put on "cosmetic weight"—carbohydrates.

Fourteen million Americans go to bed hungry every night; that is as if the total populations of Chicago and Philadelphia were combined and were all hungry.[6] To find the poor we need look no further than our poor rural areas and inner cities. (As well as in our suburbs! Twenty percent of America's poor live in the suburbs.)[7]

Another myth is that poor people are stupid or they wouldn't be poor. Poor people are no more stupid than the same percentage of the wealthier population is stupid. They simply have not been granted equality of opportunity.

Who does have a corner on opportunity in this country? What is the profile of who does and does not control the wealth?

Less than five percent of our population controls:

Fifty percent of all wealth;

Eighty-three percent of all corporate stocks;

Ninety percent of all state and local bonds;

Sixty-two percent of all business and professions.[8]

It is this less than five percent of our population which holds vested interests directly or indirectly, maliciously or non-maliciously keeping the poor poor by keeping the poor unemployed or underemployed.

What about unemployment? Approximately seven million persons are now unemployed in this country. Millions of others have part-time work because they could not find full-time work, or have given up seeking work out of discouragement. Our actual level of unemployment in this country is not the seven or eight percent the government figures show, but rather is over twelve percent.[9]

Unemployment is a vast and tragic waste of human and material resources, costing billions of dollars in lost revenue and untold amounts of increased government expenses and lost productivity.

The social and human dimension is deplorable. In his classic *Man's Search for Meaning*, Dr. Viktor Frankl compares the psychological state of the unemployed to his own state as an inmate in a World War II concentration camp. What is so devastating to the psyche of the unemployed worker, he says, is that his existence is a provisional one. It is virtually impossible for him to live for the future or aim at a goal. His suffering has no date of relief; his condition could go on forever.[10]

As for unemployment statistics, at least 12.1 million persons are unemployed or partly employed. Eight out of ten of the jobless are white. Three-fourths are adults twenty and over. The black unemployment rate is double the white (government figures).[11]

What about underemployment? Even when work is available, earnings are many times inadequate. In 1974 the heads of 2.5 million families were employed but didn't earn enough to be at the poverty level. Ten million persons were in these families.[12]

There is a segment of our population which suffers glaring and consistent underemployment. We shall take a look in the following segment at the underemployed farm worker.

There are 2.6 million American farm workers, many of whom are migrant workers who follow the harvests from the Mexican border to the state of Washington, from Texas to Michigan, from Florida to New England.[13]

Columnist Jack Anderson sent a member of his staff to Florida to infiltrate field crews of farm workers. Reporter Hal Bernton was hired to work on a tomato farm south of Naples, Florida, which was part of an international "agri-business."

His findings: Workers picked tomatoes for one cent per pound (later to be sold for up to sixty cents per pound in grocery stores). They worked in snake infested fields. The snake bite kit, which was supposed to be taken into the fields each day, lay empty in the bus that hauled the workers to the fields. On this and others of the great corporate farms, the worker earns barely enough to pay for three poor meals, a filthy mattress and a bottle of cheap wine to dull his excruciating backache. The workers are unable to pick vegetables fast enough to keep up with the charges deducted from their paychecks for room and board, and so the worker lives in virtual bondage to the straw boss. At the end of the week at least forty-two dollars was deducted from each paycheck for food alone. (My own family is able to feed two adults and two small children nutritious food each week for that amount.)

Living quarters on the farm where Bernton worked consisted of a tiny compartment (one-fourth of a battered old trailer)

which stank of wine and urine. Bernton shared his compartment
with a "bleary" companion, his cot equipped with a filthy pil-
lowless mattress.

With no heat in the winter the workers feared freezing to
death at night. The Florida Rural Legal Services finally forced
the owners to install electric heaters. The cost of the cheap heaters was deducted from the workers' pay. They were given the
dubious promise that the money would be refunded when they
turned in the heaters.

At the farm Bernton worked, the straw boss had a reputa-
tion for having beaten up troublesome workers. He had a fierce
Doberman pinscher to further help him enforce authority.

Each field hand was provided a metal pan and tin can as
personal utensils. He washed outside with no soap, thereby
passing poisonous pesticides from hand to hand and hand to
mouth. In addition the leaves of the plants laden with pesticides
rubbed against exposed hands and arms, causing some to break
out in painful rashes. In the summer the fields were invaded by
hordes of mosquitoes which stung every spot of exposed flesh,
day and night. No health care was available in the camp.

Why do they remain? Some are deeply in debt to the straw
boss. By payday, charges for living expenses have decimated
their pay. They then sign their checks over to the straw boss and
often have no money left at all. Others Bernton talked with indicated they had no hope of finding a better situation.[14]

If you were a farm worker you would be paid around one
thousand dollars a year, or if everyone in your family worked
you might earn twenty-seven hundred dollars a year. Work
would not be available on many days. Your life expectancy
would be forty-nine. Your family's chances of catching disease
would be three times the national average. You might have two
rooms for your family to live in, with no toilet, sink, bathtub, or
shower. Farm workers' children in South Carolina were found
to be getting only one-third of the normal daily caloric requirements for their age group.

Child labor thrives on the farm, although outlawed in industry in 1938. Eight hundred thousand youngsters under the

age of sixteen work in our nation's fields.[15]

A final segment on the haves and the have-nots has to do with population and resources. Our apple analogy from the hunger chapter is worth repeating here. Given ten apples, if one group has seven, the other will have three. Our resources are not unlimited. What does this tell us about population?

World population is increasing at a rate of two percent per year. This means (if this rate holds constant—and it is likely to increase) world population will double every thirty-five years.[16] "In a finite world, infinite population expansion is impossible. . . . Matching people to resources will have to stop being a slogan and become a global way of life."[17]

Birth control alone is a drop in the bucket in stabilizing population. In addition we must work at raising the status of women, reducing unemployment, improving health care especially for children, raising the level of "human capital" that a family invests in a child, and equalizing income and land distribution. It is indicated that people's fertility decreases as they gain greater control over their own lives.[18]

Our goal should be self-reliance for every human being. The key to alleviating poverty in this country (and around the world) is participation of the poor in decision-making. The people concerned must have access and power in the decision-making process within the institutions that ultimately affect their lives.[19] This is crucial in poverty areas.

It is difficult to meet the goal of alleviating poverty and affording the pursuit of happiness to every person. It is especially difficult in our big-is-better, more-is-better, faster-is-better, newer-is-better, profit-is-God society. The roots of one man's poverty are another man's greed.

(Note: Aside from the suggestion that we support international agencies which aim to relieve hunger and poverty all over the globe—UNICEF or CARE, for example—and that we act on conclusions reached from the chapter on hunger, I am confining myself in this chapter to America's poor. It would take an entire volume to record America's role in keeping the poor of other countries poor.)

II. Study Bibliography

"Appalachia." *Gamaliel.* Volume 2, Number 1. Community for Creative Nonviolence: Washington, D.C., Spring, 1976.

"Justice in the World." Synod of Bishops. United States Catholic Conference: Washington, D.C., 1971.

Poverty in American Democracy: A Study of Social Power. Campaign for Human Development. United States Catholic Conference: Washington, D.C., 1975.

Poverty Profile. Campaign for Human Development. United States Catholic Conference: Washington, D.C., 1972.

"This Land Is Home to Me." Pastoral of the Catholic Bishops of Appalachia. Contained in *Flesh and Spirit: A Religious View of Bicentennial America.* Community for Creative Nonviolence: Washington, D.C., 1976. (Order from Gamaliel, 1335 N Street, N.W., Washington, D.C. 20005, checks payable to Gamaliel.)

III. Reflections as a Christian

To be a person of Christian integrity means that Jesus' Word is one with our deeds. Word, creed and deed should be one for us. The moral schizophrenia that has plagued many Christians and their institutions must come to an end. To say one thing and live another thing can lead to nothing but destruction for the individual Christian and suffocation for Christian communities. When we profess concern for the poor but do not integrate this concern into our active Christian life we are laughing in the face of the healing message of Jesus and fooling no one but ourselves.

This chapter thus far has been largely concerned with material poverty. Economic tyranny sees those who oppress others (out of greed or unconcern) as the worse off, morally speaking.

Throughout his life Jesus urged us to be poor: "Happy are the poor in spirit" (Mt. 5:3). What did he mean? Louis Evely in his remarkable reflection *That Man Is You* presents the finest treatise on spiritual poverty that I have ever come across. He says that material poverty is an economic condition, not a virtue. To aspire to it is not necessarily to gain in virtue. Poverty first begins when we renounce our concept of poverty.

Evely says:

> We habitually deceive ourselves in one of two ways. "I'm not attached to anything," we maintain; "therefore, I can keep everything. I'm poor at heart." Or we declare: "I deprive myself of a lot of things that my father had, that my neighbor owns or that my friend, who says he's such a good Christian, hasn't given up. So I've a perfect right to talk poverty to others." No, we've merely preferred a spiritual possession to a material one. And that's worse. We should hurry up and buy what we've sacrificed and relinquish our right to preach to anyone. The humiliation of being rich is a first step toward poverty, whereas pride in one's poverty is the most dangerous of luxuries. "I thank you that I'm not like this publican" can easily become "I thank you that I'm not like this Pharisee."[1]

Evely offers a few tests to tell whether we are indeed poor in spirit. A few of these points follow.

(1) Do we sing the Magnificat when the Lord cuts our moorings materially or spiritually?

(2) How do we feel when he asks us to change? (not the time of our daily prayers but our whole way of looking at a situation or person)

(3) Can we get out of our egos?

(4) Can we learn to really listen to something besides ourselves because we know we'd never be able to manage alone?

(5) Are we willing to be reproved, tormented and driven out of ourselves by the voice of God?

(6) For God's sake would we be willing to leave belongings, country, heritage, culture, our ways and our past?

(7) Are we willing to unfetter ourselves from the riches of

peace, comfort, security, privacy, and independence if we are too attached to them?[2]

If we can say "Praise the Lord!" when God continually pulls the rug out from under us and says "Surprise!" then we have a measure of spiritual poverty. But let's not be too pleased with our resiliency and openness or we will find ourselves possessed again. "God wants us to keep nothing," Evely says, "so he can give us everything."[3]

Let us not confuse Jesus' desire for us to be spiritually poor with his wanting the poor to continue in their deprivation. When Jesus says in Mark 14:7, "You have the poor with you always," he is not striking up the band for the status quo economically speaking. He is rather contrasting the "continuance of it [poverty] with his own fleeting presence among men."[4] Jesus' life-style and message witness to his active concern for those in need both spiritually and materially. Do ours?

Scripture Passages for Reflection

Leviticus 25:35-39
Deuteronomy 15:9-11
Ezekiel 18:12; 22:29
Matthew 6:20
Mark 10:21
Luke 12:33; 18:22
Acts 4:34-35
1 John 3:17-18

IV. Questions for Reflection/Discussion

(1) Does our economic society really reflect the moral ideal of democracy?

(2) How does the spirit of competition which pervades American life hurt the poor or help the poor?

(3) In the United States, economic benefit and sharing the society's wealth are primarily tied to ownership of productive

resources. What does this mean for the poor?

(4) How do self-sufficiency and individualism stack up in light of the teachings of Jesus Christ and his Church?

(5) What is success?

(6) How do our society's goals of material success and pleasure affect the poor and our efforts at relieving the poverty-stricken?

(7) How does the stress put on high productivity and maximum efficiency effect the employment picture?

V. Suggested Actions

(1) Contribute your expertise (legal, medical, plumbing, dietary or whatever) to the poor.[1]

(2) Start a food pantry for emergency food for the poor in a given area.

(3) Assist your county or state health officials in disseminating health care (free or low cost) information to the poor.

(4) Provide transportation to get the needy to these clinics.

(5) Establish and publicize a referral office with information on where the poor can get help. This can be a telephone-only operation, with phone or phones manned around the clock.

(6) Found a day care center so needy mothers can afford to work.

(7) Found a pre-school or kindergarten.

(8) Help the poor to exercise political rights by aiding in voter registration and providing transportation to the polls.

(9) Pay a *living* wage to those in your hire—regardless of the "status" of their job.

(10) Volunteer to tutor in poverty area programs.[2]

(11) "Adopt" a needy family and let them "adopt" you. Share with each other your unique riches. (This is being done with success by individual families in the New Orleans charismatic renewal movement.)

(12) Resist media advertising for unnecessary goods and foods. Give the money saved to those who need it.

(13) Write your congresspersons in support of the minimum wage being extended to cover *all* jobs.

(14) Join in efforts to reverse migration from inner cities to suburbs.

Ways to help the farm workers specifically were suggested in the *Christopher News Notes*:

(15) Support legislation that affords farm workers the protections that other workers have.

(16) Arrange for talks on farm worker conditions to your organizations, churches, schools, and home meetings.

(17) Write letters to the editor in support of farm workers' rights.

(18) Boycott California grapes and iceberg (head) lettuce.

(19) Help your local boycott committee or organize one of your own.

(20) Raise the issue of the boycott at supermarkets, restaurants and wherever else grapes and lettuce are served or sold.[3]

Other Suggestions

(21) Encourage raising the status of women.[4]

(22) Support reducing unemployment.

(23) Support improved health care.

(24) Support equalizing land distribution.

(25) Support equalizing of income.

(26) Reorder your life so that you have time to participate in the regeneration of moral sensitivity in your family, community, country, and world.[5]

(27) Study the materials listed in the study bibliography and judge how you and your group can best help those who are barely surviving.

(28) Support the overhaul of housing programs for the poor and working poor so that they may have a decent place to live and a rent they can afford.

(29) Support governmental full employment policies.

(30) Work for fairness in taxation.
(31) Support a decent income policy for those unable to work.
(32) Educate yourself and your group to issues of economic justice.
(33) Pray.

10
RACE RELATIONS

There are two races of men in this world . . . the "race" of the decent man and the "race" of the indecent man. Both are found everywhere; they penetrate into all groups of society.

Viktor E. Frankl

I. Introduction

I recall a conversation I had in 1964 with a black friend of mine in the Young Christian Student movement. We were walking down a Chicago street after a series of YCS business meetings which had taken place that day at the national office. Much of the day had been spent writing social inquiries on the themes of social justice, and our conversation was about justice in the United States at that time. In making a point I referred to the United States as "our country," and he pulled me up short. He said, "This may be your country, Sheila, but it isn't mine." Through no fault of his own, my friend was indeed a nominal citizen of this country. He was a citizen in name only, with only the words and precious few of the freedoms and privileges that accompanied my own citizenship. I have never forgotten nor let myself forget what my friend said.

The examples used in this introduction will refer mainly to black/white race relations. The definition of racism and the nature of prejudice apply to all those persons and groups we oppress in this country, be they black, chicano, native American, Puerto Rican, Chinese American, and so forth.

The specifics of racism and its specific effects are different for each minority and for each individual within each minority. Further differences, as well as some similarities, are seen in different areas of the country, different areas within our cities, and geographically different rural areas.

What is racism? "Racism is any attitude, action, or institutional structure which subordinates a person or group because of his or their color."[1]

Racism falls basically into two categories: overt racism of individuals and groups toward those of a different race, and institutional racism, which is a kind of indirect subordination of those of a different color. Overt racism is like a dead branch; institutional racism is like a tree which is diseased.

An example of overt racism would be the refusal of an individual landlord to rent to a person solely because he is a certain color. An example of institutional racism is given in the United States Commission on Civil Rights report, *Racism in America and How To Combat It*:

> [An example is] the widely used practice of denying employment to applicants with any non-traffic police record because this tends to discriminate unfairly against residents of low-income areas where police normally arrest young men for minor incidents that are routinely overlooked in wealthy suburbs.[2]

This last example reveals layers of institutional racism. The reason the minority is in the poorer area in the first place has to do with discrimination in the areas of education and employment, not to mention housing.

To be on the receiving end of overt racism is like being directly kicked in the teeth by another more or less identifiable human being. To be on the receiving end of institutional racism, on the other hand, is like being kicked in the teeth again and again by a computer or by "City Hall." In terms of the latter, neither blacks nor whites working for interracial justice know immediately just who is responsible for the atrocities. They are the aggregate result in many cases of hundreds of years of institutionally condoned racism.

How far have we come since striking down legalized racism (at least in theory) one hundred years ago? Social researchers at the University of Michigan tell us that in 1964 strict segregation was favored by twenty-five percent of the whites. In 1974 strict segregation was favored by only ten percent of the whites. Although whites perceived a real change in the position of blacks in the first part of the 1970's, blacks were less positive about this point.[3]

United States Census Bureau figures are less than positive about the real gains for the black person in our country. According to 1974 Bureau of the Census figures, of the total white population twenty-five years of age and older, roughly twenty-seven percent had finished high school. Of the total black population in the same age range, roughly eighteen and a half percent had finished high school. Of the total white population twenty-five years of age and older, approximately six percent had completed four years of college. Of the total black population in the same age range, only three percent had completed four years of college. So much for equality of educational opportunity.

How does the employment picture look for blacks today? Census figures show that as of 1974, the mean income of white males age twenty-five and older was $11,370 per year. The mean income of black males in the same age range was $6,793 per year.[4]

The major paper I wrote as a high school senior in the early 1960's was titled, "A Wall Is His Horizon: A Study of the Opportunities of the American Negro in the Fields of Education and Employment." Yes, things have improved since that time, but by how much?

The reason the disease called racism is still with us is that the oppressor benefits (economically, politically, psychologically) from it. If he or she did not "benefit" from this imagined superiority over others, racism would soon be a thing of the past.

In order to heal race relations which have been sorely broken, it is not enough to desegregate, i.e., to drop the barriers to equality of opportunity. In addition we must integrate, i.e., we must overcome the effects of prolonged repression of minority group members. The United States Commission on Civil Rights considers the following conditions necessary for two groups to consider themselves integrated:

Enough members of both groups are *actually present* so that everyone in the situation constantly perceives both groups in day-to-day experience.

Enough members of the minority group in that situation (who might be white) are present so that as individuals they do not feel isolated or lost within the majority group.

The minority-group in that situation exercises power and influence at least proportional to its numbers there. . . .

Integration . . . requires *actual mixing* of these groups on a daily basis. That is one reason why integration implies positive programs rather than just the removal of discriminatory barriers.

It further states:

Effective integration . . . is often inhibited because such a high proportion of . . . minority groups live in segregated areas. Thus, achieving significant integration implies much greater Negro movement into now predominantly white residential areas. . . . This seems out of favor with many minority group leaders seeking . . . solidarity and political power through group concentration.[5]

Yet, it concludes, without effective integration we will have separate societies. Separate societies cannot be equal, especially in the area of economic opportunity.

In light of the present situation, what can we do to realize liberation for oppressed races? I put this question to a friend and expert in the field of race relations, G. Joseph Putnam. Speaking of the black struggle, he indicated to me that a concerned white should first study, reflect, and work on overcoming himself and his own racist cultural baggage:

[Then] at least he won't be doing any harm. His first and primary objective should be . . . helping himself to overcome all the racist feelings, thoughts, attitudes and reflexes with which he has been impregnated from the first moment of his existence. This alone will be a long and traumatic experience for him. It will require going into the black community to be helped rather than to help. And it will require coming out of the black community to confront the rest of the white community. It will require an unrelenting battle to either convert or destroy and dismantle white racist institutions. (Some are so racist that destruction is the only answer.) It will require doing this in collaboration with blacks *and* other whites. He will have to be specific. He will have to pick a particular point of entry into the black world, preferably with reference to his own professional or work background. He will have to pick one or more specific white institutions, preferably one of those he has some ties to. When he begins to deal with the problem . . . he will begin to realize what black people have had to deal with all their lives.

Mr. Putnam further stated:

He will then begin to understand that blacks are quite capable of taking care of themselves if only whites would stop burying them in racist. . . . He will realize that the best contribution he can make is to attack the . . . slingers. Then he's going to find himself buried in the stuff too. If he is still with us after he digs himself out a couple of times, then I believe he is ready to help black people. Now he won't have to ask, it will come second nature to him. At this point, he will be ready to become a part of the struggle for black liberation.[6]

Whites first must challenge themselves. After that, one of the major ways that whites can help blacks and other oppressed minorities is to challenge their own white communities. Another way is to support the blacks and minorities in their own work to free themselves.

II. Study Bibliography

Billingsley, Andrew. *Black Families in White America*. Prentice Hall, Inc.: Englewood Cliffs, N.J., 1968.

Cleaver, Eldridge. *Soul on Ice.* McGraw-Hill: New York, 1967.

Coser, Lewis. *The Functions of Social Conflict.* Free Press: Glencoe, Illinois, 1956.

Cox, Fred M. *et al. Strategies of Community Organization.* F. E. Peacock: Itasca, Ill., 1970.

Dillard, J. L. *Black English.* Random House: New York, 1972.

Fairbairn, Ann. *Five Smooth Stones.* Crown Publishers: New York, 1966.

Frazier, Thomas. *Underside of American History.* Harcourt, Brace, Jovanovich, Inc.: New York, 1971.

Graham, James. *The Enemies of the Poor.* Random House: New York, 1970.

Harris, Thomas A., M.D. *I'm OK—You're OK.* Harper and Row: New York, 1969.

Liebow, Elliot. *Tally's Corner.* Little, Brown: Boston, 1967.

Rubin, Theodore, M.D. *The Angry Book.* Macmillan: New York, 1969.

Rudwick, Elliot and Meier, August. *From Plantation to Ghetto.* Hill and Wang: New York, 1966.

Yette, Samuel F. *The Choice: Black Survival in America.* Putnam: New York, 1971.

III. Reflections as a Christian

In the first incarnation described in Genesis 1:26-27, God creates mankind in his own image and likeness. In the second incarnation God incarnates Jesus of Nazareth, a deeply brown-skinned Jewish lay person from the Middle East. This Jew preaches that there are no longer to be any inequalities between persons in God's eyes. Regardless of social class, nationality, race, sex, or religion, all persons are worthy of God acting in their lives (grace). All persons are worthy of our loving service. Through Christ and signified by our baptism, we are all made heirs equally to the promise of God made to Abraham.

This young Jewish man tells us that heaven is for the peacemakers and the persecuted. It would seem, then, that heaven is not for the persecutors nor for their accomplices—those who stand by and do nothing. He asks us, "Why do you call me, 'Lord, Lord,' and not do what I say. . . . The one who listens and does nothing is like the man who built his house on soil, with no foundations: as soon as the river bore down on it, it collapsed; and what a ruin the house becomes" (Luke 6:46, 49).

We are called to minister not only to the wounds of the oppressed, but to the open sores of the oppressors. I have often thought of how much easier it is to help out a member of a minority group who is downtrodden than to confront a white racist community and its institutions. I have always found it much easier to love the black person lying in the gutter who is being kicked by a gang of whites than to love the gang of whites doing the kicking. Yet this is precisely what Jesus asks of us: "You have learned how it was said: *You must love your neighbor* and hate your enemy. But I say this to you: love your enemies, pray for your persecutors. In this way you will be sons of your Father in heaven, for he causes his sun to rise on bad men as well as good, and his rain to fall on honest and dishonest men alike. For if you love those who love you, what right have you to claim any credit? Even the tax collectors do as much, do they not? And if you save your greetings for your brothers, are you doing anything exceptional? Even the pagans do as much, do they not? You must therefore be perfect just as your heavenly Father is perfect" (Mt. 5:43-48). So to be truly Christ-like we must, as Gary Chamberlain says, realize that "the Church's mission task calls it to deal not only with the injustices of minority peoples but also with the spiritual wounds of the white majority."[1]

We can legitimately call ourselves into question over the effects of both overt racism and institutional racism. Overt racism is personal sin for which we as individuals may be responsible. Institutional racism is social sin which we as individuals are responsible for perpetuating. In our reflections concerning our own culpability in institutional racism, it might help to reflect on the description of social sin rendered by the Campaign for Human Development:

1. Social structures that oppress human beings, vio-

late human dignity, stifle freedom, impose gross in-
equality.
2. Situations that promote and facilitate individual
acts of selfishness.
3. The complicity of persons who do not take responsibility for the evil being done.[2]

For those of us who follow the rules to the letter but go no
further, for those of us who offer civility to the oppressed but
offer it in place of justice, for those of us who hide out in our
own felicitous communities while the persecutors and the defilers have their reign, we should count on being vomited out of
the mouth of the Lord like so much warm milk.

Scripture Passages for Reflection

Luke 10:29-37
Mark 3:31-35
Mark 10:42-45
Mark 12:28-34
1 Corinthians 12:12-14
Galatians 3:26-28

IV. Questions for Reflection/Discussion

(1) Is it Christian for white people to look down on black people? For Catholics to look down on non-Catholics? For
charismatics to look down on non-charismatics? For priests
to look down on the laity? Is a feeling of superiority essentially a Christian feeling? What is elitism?
(2) What is positive about the melting pot idea popular in times
past to describe the make-up of American society? What is
negative about the phrase's meaning?
(3) Sociologist Andrew Greeley prefers the term "stew pot" to
describe the American experience. Do you think this is a
preferable description? Why? Why not?
(4) Justice involves more than neighborliness and civility. On

what deeper levels does Christian "neighborliness" operate?

(5) What specifically can society (its institutions and individuals) do to treat you fairly and with active concern? In your job? In your church community?

(6) How can you and your group make the values brought out in question 5 work for others?

V. Suggested Actions

(1) Take a racist to lunch. He or she needs your help more than the minority groups do. (The minority groups need you to help get him or her off their backs.)

(2) Find out from your local patrolman what the proportion of police protection is in your neighborhood compared to that in poorer minority group neighborhoods. Then challenge the higher-ups in the police department to justify this distribution of services.

(3) Read and do group study work on any or all of the books in the study bibliography (section II).

(4) Support direct participation by the private sector in remedial programs for low income minority group areas. Such programs might include education, job creation, training, housing, and even welfare administration.

(5) Find out what "red lining" is in the real estate business, and decide on what you and your group can do about it.

(6) Raise money and send it to: The United Negro College Fund, 55 E. 52nd Street, New York, N.Y. 10022.

(7) Found a scholarship fund at a local college for minority students.

(8) If you are an employer, pay the same fair wage to those who do the same work. Urge other employers in your prayer group and parish to do likewise.

(9) Find out if the company you work for engages in fair hiring and wage practices. If they do not, they are breaking the law.

(10) Organize a seminar for your prayer group, parish, or neighborhood community on the subject of racism.

(11) Ask members of minorities what you and your group can do to help combat racism. *Listen* to what they have to say.

(12) Raise money and purchase good books on the subject of race relations for your church, school, or city library.

(13) The U.S. Commission on Civil Rights suggests that we support the generation of Negro economic resources by encouraging Negroes to "direct their consumer trade and other business to Negro-operated stores, banks, service firms, professional firms, restaurants, etc. Clearly, such behavior involves taking race and color into account in making decisions; hence some might consider it 'black racism.' But it can more accurately be viewed as a form of 'black pride.' "

(14) Support black businesses and other minority group businesses, regardless of your color.

Addendum to Suggested Action List

In its booklet *Racism in America and How To Combat It*, the U.S. Commission on Civil Rights offers nine strategies for combating racism. They are:

1. Make all Americans—especially whites—far more conscious of the widespread existence of racism in all its forms, and the immense costs it imposes on the entire nation . . . economic . . . political . . . social and human costs. . . . It is impossible to quantify these costs . . . [but] for example, in 1965, if Negro families had received the same average income as whites, incomes received by all U.S. families would have been $15.7 billion higher. The process of education necessary to change white perceptions . . . must involve . . . various groups of whites [who] thoroughly examine their own behavior in order to uncover all the subtle and unconscious forms of racism embedded in it. . . . Whites must overcome their habitual exclusion of Negroes and other minority group members in this process of self-examination.

2. Build up capabilities of minority group members, and greatly strengthen their opportunities and power

to exercise those capabilities, especially regarding public and private activities that directly affect them. . . .
An essential ingredient is expressing strong political
support for key national policies concerning housing,
education, civil rights, employment, welfare programs,
tax reforms, and other measures with antiracist effects. . . . Until such white political support is both
created and forcefully expressed to Congressional representatives, no effective nationwide attack on racism
is possible. . . . In primarily Negro areas, this strategy is closely related to the concepts of "Black Power"
and "Black Nationalism," but it need not involve support of geographic separatism. . . . One important
device for developing Negro and other minority group
business capabilities is the "third-party contract" for
providing both public and private services. For in-
stance, if expanded government services concerning
neighborhood maintenance were to be carried out, the
local government could contract that function in mainly Negro areas to a Negro-owned and operated firm
organized for that purpose, rather than enlarging the
government itself.

One of the objectives of this basic strategy is to equip
Negroes and other minority group leaders with much
greater bargaining power in dealing with whites. . . .

3. Develop legislative and other programs which si-
multaneously provide benefits for significant parts of
the white majority and for deprived or other members
of nonwhite minority groups, so it will be in the immediate self-interest of the former to support programs
to aid the latter. . . . There are two important qualifi-
cations to this strategy. First, such programs will not
improve the *relative* position of the minority groups
concerned unless they provide larger benefits to those
groups than to members of the middle class majority
they also aid. . . . This leads to the second qualifica-
tion: it is virtually impossible to create programs

which provide *net* benefits both to most severely deprived people and to most of the middle class white majority. . . . However, programs can be devised which provide net benefits to most of the lowest-income group and to large segments of the middle-income group.

4. Insure that minority group members are in a position to contribute to the design, execution, and evaluation of all major social policies and programs. This will improve the quality of such policies and programs by introducing a certain sensitivity to human values which is too often lacking in the overly technology-oriented behavior of the white majority.

5. Influence local, state, and national policies and programs—both public and private—so they have certain characteristics which will reduce their possible racist effects. . . . Avoid any action or arrangement that unnecessarily produces, sustains, or emphasizes derogatory or stigmatizing forms of differentiation. . . . For example, current public housing regulations require that all the families living in a public housing project have very low incomes. This tends to stigmatize such projects as undesirable. . . . Conceivably, public housing projects could contain a majority of stable moderate-income families. . . . Similarly, locating all the public housing projects in a city (except those for the elderly) so that nearly all occupants are Negroes has racist effects. . . .

[Have] emphasis upon participation by, and within, the private sector rather than direct dependency upon government at any level. . . . It is vital that society avoid creating low-income minority group neighborhoods that are almost totally dependent upon direct public expenditures aimed at self-maintenance, rather than at producing services consumed by society as a whole. . . . Use . . . a metropolitan areawide geographic focus whenever possible.

6. Create recognition among all Americans that overcoming the burdens of racism will cost a great deal of money, time, effort, and institutional change, but that this cost is a worthwhile investment in the future which both society as a whole and individual taxpayers can bear without undue strain.

7. Search out and develop alliances of nonwhites and whites organized to obtain common practical goals, particularly in combating racism.

8. Create many more positively oriented contacts between whites and Negroes and other minority group members—including personal contacts, intergroup contacts, and those occurring through mass media.

9. Open up many more opportunities for minority group members in now predominantly white organizations (such as businesses), areas (such as suburban neighborhoods), or institutions (such as public schools), and encourage other arrangements where members of different groups work, live, or act together.

11
ADDENDUM

I. Consumerism

A highly amusing friend of mine named Pat likes to tell me that she no longer prays to God for help in her daily comings and goings. "I pray directly to Ralph Nader," she says, "and eliminate the middleman!"

All kidding aside, it would be wise for your group to acquaint itself with the work of consumer advocates. Consumer education is an idea whose time has come.

Your group might find the following to be good sources of information on this topic:

Consumer Education Bibliography. Office of Consumer Affairs, Executive Office Building, Washington, D.C. 20506.

Dorfman, John. *Consumer Survival Kit.* Praeger, 1975.

Nader, Ralph (ed.). *The Consumer and Corporate Accountability.* Harcourt, Brace, Jovanovich, Inc.: New York 1973.

There follows a social inquiry which will serve as a starting point for your group in consumer affairs.

OBSERVE
1. What consumer agencies are available to serve you at the city and state level?
2. Is there an effective ombudsman in your city government to whom you have recourse when city services fail?
3. What services does your local Better Business Bureau offer to consumers?
4. How is your town's public service utilities system using your energy?
5. Is adequate public transit available?
6. Cite some examples of monopolies in our country (or in your local community), if monopoly is defined in terms of the four largest firms in a given industry controlling fifty percent of the market or more.

JUDGE
1. Should monopolies exist in a Christian society?
2. Reflect on the meaning of John 17:17 and Ephesians 4:14-15.

ACT
1. As a group, read *The Consumer and Corporate Accountability*. Discuss its implications.
2. As a prayer group organize seminars on consumer affairs for the various parishes to which you belong.
3. Start a consumer affairs club with the purpose of providing consumer education to the elderly or others in particular need.
4. Write to some or all of the agencies listed below. Use the materials you receive to set up exhibitions of consumer information at banks, schools, libraries, elderly persons' centers, etc.

Helps and Resources
1. Consumer Product Safety Commission
   7315 Wisconsin Ave., N.W.
   Washington, D.C. 20016
2. Consumers Union of the U.S.
   256 Washington Street
   Mount Vernon, N.Y. 10550
3. Department of Agriculture
   14th Street and Independence Ave., S.E.
   Washington, D.C. 20250
4. Department of Commerce
   14th Street between Constitution Ave.
      & E St., N.W.
   Washington, D.C. 20203
5. Federal Trade Commission
   Pennsylvania Ave. at Sixth St., N.W.
   Washington, D.C. 20580
6. Food and Drug Administration
   5600 Fishers Lane
   Rockville, Md. 20852

7. National Consumers League
   1785 Massachusetts Ave.
   Washington, D.C. 20036
8. National Highway Traffic Safety
   Administration
   400 Seventh St., S.W.
   Washington, D.C. 20591
9. Office of Consumer Affairs
   New Executive Office Building
   Washington, D.C. 20506
10. Office of Economic Opportunity
    1200 Nineteenth St., N.W.
    Washington, D.C. 20506
11. Ralph Nader Center for Study of
    Responsive Law
    P.O. Box 19367
    Washington, D.C. 20036

II. Education

In my original outline for this book, the topic of "education" was to receive a full chapter. In doing research I discovered that even minimal coverage of the topic would fill two volumes. The following are the two volumes I suggest you and your group look into:

Postman, Neil, and Weingartner, Charles. *The School Book.* Delacorte Press: New York, 1973.
Silberman, Charles E. *Crisis in the Classroom: The Remaking of American Education.* Random House: New York, 1970.

With regard to definition of terms, keep in mind that "education" is not synonymous with "schools," and that in a great number of instances the two are mutually exclusive. Further, keep in mind what one sage at my college passed on to me. She said that the goal of education should be to engage students in the process of critical thinking. If a student graduates with a cum laude degree but is not yet a critical thinker, he is not truly educated. (It follows—perish the thought—that one could possibly become a critical thinker with little formal education!)

The following are social inquiries concerning education which you and your group can do. They, and the inquiries in the following pages on political action, peace, and housing, are adapted from *Social Inquiries for Parish Christian Service Committees* published by the Social Action Department of the Diocese of Davenport, Iowa, which is under the able direction of Rev. Marvin A. Mottet.

PUBLIC SCHOOLS

OBSERVE
1. Does your public school teach courses in the civil liberties of U.S. citizens? Does it teach a course in civil rights? Is the school board an equal-opportunity employer?
2. Is your school district desegregated? Do minorities and whites both receive quality education? Are there minorities teaching on the staff? Are minorities represented on your school board in proportion to their population in your area?
3. Are there any Catholics on the school board?
4. Are there "shared-time" arrangements between the public and Catholic schools in your area?
5. Is there multi-cultural education in your public school district?
6. Are social studies taught from a "global family" perspective in your district? Are the economic and political realities of the Third World taught in your school?
7. Does your public school reinforce tendencies toward excessive competition, money-making, chauvinism, nationalism (to an inordinate degree), racism, sexism?
8. How is discipline handled in your public school? How are teachers hired and fired?
9. Does your school board give equal service to private school students in auxiliary services?

10. Is "my country right or wrong" preached at your public school? Do the students learn how our political system works?

JUDGE

1. What one thing would you recommend that your public school stop doing in order to improve the educational atmosphere of the school?
2. What one thing would you recommend that your public school *start* doing?
3. Where do "values" fit in public education?

ACT

1. Run for the local school board or regularly attend its meetings.
2. Find out the answers to some of the above questions and push for change, if you judge it is needed.
3. Work toward community control of your school.
4. Find out about multi-cultural education in your area and work for its implementation in your school.
5. Work to get public aid to private education through your legislature. Contact your representatives and senators on the state and federal level.

CATHOLIC SCHOOLS

OBSERVE

1. Do you know whether your Catholic school has made a commitment to implement social justice into its life-style and curriculum?
2. Do you know what resource books are used to teach Christian social justice attitudes to your children?
3. Is there a Christian service course required in the curriculum of your school?
4. Do you know the discipline policy in your school?
5. Do you know the wage scale and hiring and firing practices of your school? Are teachers required to have background and training in social justice education?

6. What (if any) parental input is there into the operation and style of the school?
7. How does the parents' organization function?
8. How does the school service the community at large?
9. Is your school "different where it counts" in terms of the Christian moral conscience of your children?
10. Does your school help or hinder racial integration?
11. Does your school educate primarily the more affluent Catholics, or is there a broad spectrum of economic levels in the school?
12. Are you as parents aiding in the social justice education of your children by being models, by influencing behaviors, attitudes, and values, and by showing how to practice social justice?
13. Has anyone reviewed the books used in your Catholic schools to discover whether they contain racist and sexist language or attitudes?
14. Do graduates of your Catholic school seem to be critical thinkers in the best sense of the term?

JUDGE

1. How should Catholic schools be "different where it counts"?
2. Do Vatican II and World Synod '71 throw any light on this?
3. Reflect on 1 John 1:3.
4. What do the U.S. bishops teach in *To Teach as Jesus Did*?

ACT

1. Join the school board of education and push for implementation of social justice teaching in your school.
2. Read *Justice in the World*, the statement of the World Synod of Bishops, 1971. Decide on specific ways to implement principles that would have an uplifting effect on your Catholic school.

III. Government and Politics

Jimmy Breslin supplies the introductory remarks to this mini-section:

> Now religion ought to have more to do than just with Sunday. How can you not work in this political system and be a practicing Catholic? That's something that always puzzles me, that people can't see the connection between being a Catholic and being interested in government. You know that one Jewish election district is worth ten Irish election districts in a primary campaign. There'll be more Jewish people come out to vote in one district than in ten of the Irish Catholic districts. That means they don't know how important it is to try to do something about the conditions that hurt and oppress people. . . . Politics is a very high calling. It really is the life of Christ if you get right down to it. How else can we do anything about the world's problems?
>
> "A Day With Jimmy Breslin"
by Eugene Kennedy

In other words, unless the Lord watch the city . . . (cf. Psalm 27).

The Illinois Bell Telephone Company put out a very helpful list of things to remember when writing to your representatives:

1. Identify yourself.
2. Be informed on the subject.
3. Be brief and to the point.
4. Tell him what you think he should do if the matter is pending legislation.
5. Never send a form letter.
6. Write to the representative from your district or state. He is the one who can help you.

7. Never send a carbon when writing to more than one representative.
8. Thank your representative for something he (or she) has done which pleases you.
9. Write more than one letter; keep your representative informed of your views.

How and Where To Address Public Officials

United States Senator

Envelope: The Honorable . . .
Senate Office Building
Washington, D.C. 20510
Salutation: Dear Senator . . .

United States Representative

Envelope: The Honorable . . .
House Office Building
Washington, D.C. 20515
Salutation: Dear Mr., Ms., or Miss . . .

State Senator

Envelope: The Honorable . . .
State Capitol
Your Capital City, Your State
Salutation: Dear Senator . . .

State Representative

Envelope: The Honorable . . .
State Capitol
Your Capital City, Your State
Salutation: Dear Mr., Ms., or Miss . . .

The following two social inquiries on political action and peace may assist your group in getting started in this area.

NOTE: Don't afford yourself the luxury of tiring of making waves in the larger community. Remember, we are to emulate Jesus, and Jesus rocked the boat unto death.

POLITICAL ACTION

OBSERVE

1. Who are your city, school board, county, state, and national elected officials?
2. Do you know the process by which they are nominated and elected? The platforms on which they run?
3. Do you have some idea of the responsibilities you entrust to them? Some way to measure their performance?
4. Are the members of your parish and prayer group registered to vote? *Do* they vote?
5. Do members of your parish and prayer group hold positions in the local and national political parties?
6. Given our present constitutional system, should alternative processes for the nomination and election of public officials be developed?
7. Is the inherent dignity of each person and his freedom from oppression best preserved by the present processes for nomination and election?

JUDGE

1. What obligations does a Christian have in regard to the election of elected officials?
2. What is the teaching of papal social encyclicals and Vatican Council II in this regard?
3. Reflect on John 17.

ACT

1. Encourage qualified Christian persons to seek out political office; support those persons.
2. Encourage qualified Christian persons to involve themselves in the political parties.
3. Establish monitor teams which will appraise the platforms and performances of elected officials.
4. Work in voter registration drives and then actually assist people to get to the polls on election day.

Helps and Sources

1. Your local League of Women Voters.
2. Local Democratic and Republican parties.

3. Local elected officials.
4. Pope Paul's *A Call to Action.*
5. The 1971 World Synod of Bishops' *Justice in the World.*
6. Catholics for Christian Political Action, 1609 K St., N.W., Washington, D.C. 20006.

PEACE

OBSERVE

1. What is being done in your parish, prayer group and community to enhance the cause of world peace?
2. What do you think are the causes of violence in the world?
3. How do you personally define "peace"?
4. Are non-violent conflict resolution skills taught to the youth of your community—in your homes, churches, and schools?
5. What does the term "institutional violence" mean to you? Are there examples of it in your home, city, state, nation, or global community?
6. How do economic conditions affect chances for peace in the world?
7. What does your church community do to celebrate the dignity and ultimate value of all human life in its liturgies and other communal events?
8. What percent of the U.S. budget is spent directly on peacemaking activities?
9. How do the schools in your area promote the cause of world peace?
10. How do people in your community view the citizens of Communist countries?

JUDGE

1. What is the difference between justice as understood in the New Testament sense and the legal meaning of the term used in civil society?
2. What is the Gospel teaching on a Christian being a peace-maker? Reflect on Matthew 5:1-12.

3. What do you think your parish, prayer group, and diocese can do to teach and do peacemaking on a local, state, national, and international level? Reflect on the U.S. bishops' 1971 statement on *Justice in the World.*

4. Examine your attitudes on violence—when it is permissible and when it is not—in light of Jesus' attitude and actions when violence was done to him (his passion and crucifixion). Reflect on the passion of Jesus in Luke 23:32-49. Reflect on Matthew 21:12.

ACT

1. Investigate joining the Fellowship of Reconciliation, Box 271, Nyack, N.Y. 10960, and the Catholic Peace Fellowship, 339 Lafayette Street, New York, N.Y. 10012.

2. Work to have the schools in your city teach the students how to resolve conflict non-violently, how to see themselves as world citizens, and how to analyze world problems from a perspective of a global community.

3. Support political candidates who promote world peace and true justice.

4. Work for a peace studies program in your local school.

5. Support the United Nations as a world body which is to solve international problems non-violently.

6. Investigate Planetary Citizenship. Write Planetary Citizens, 777 United Nations Plaza, New York, N.Y. 10017.

Resources

1. Peace Consultant, National Catholic Education Association, 1730 Grove Street, Berkeley, Cal. 94709.

2. Peace and Justice Consultant, National Federation of Priests' Councils, 1307 S. Wabash, Chicago, Ill. 60605.

3. *Education for Justice, A Resource Manual*, ed. by Thomas P. Fenton, Orbis Books: Maryknoll, N.Y. 10545.

4. *Education for Peace and Justice*, a resource manual from the Institute for the Education to Peace and Justice, 3700 W. Pine Blvd., St. Louis, Mo. 63108.

5. Public Action Coalition on Toys (PACT), P.O. Box 189, Providence, Utah 84332, a consumer watchdog which ad-

vocates good toys and works to stop toys that injure, exploit, or produce attitudes of war and violence.

IV. Housing

Two problems immediately come to mind in the area of housing. The first has to do with city services to subsidized housing, and the second has to do with the practice of "red-lining" by lending institutions.

In a city which shall remain nameless but which I am certain is not unique, there is a wildly disproportionate distribution of police protection depending on the neighborhood in which you live.

This past summer I had the opportunity to interview a patrolman who came to me concerned about this situation. The tourist district of the city in question as well as the neighborhoods of the more affluent got heavy police protection. The housing projects were virtually without service.

One patrolman told me that on most occasions he and his partner are the only patrolmen on duty to cover two to three housing projects for a twelve hour shift. Population of the projects is approximately 15,000 to 17,000 persons per project. On one occasion there were only two policemen assigned to *four* housing projects, one of which is a great distance out of the city.

"Red-lining" is an unofficially practiced policy of discrimination by banks and other lending institutions. These institutions are more than willing to receive deposits of money from persons in any area of a city. But when it comes to lending money to these and other citizens (who otherwise comply with the necessary conditions for a loan) for either home improvements or for a mortgage, the institution says "no" because of the area in which the property is located. "Red-lining" occurs most often in "changing" neighborhoods. The policy serves as a self-fulfilling prophecy for the downgrading of a neighborhood. With no money being lent to people who wish to purchase and/or improve property in the area, it soon develops into a slum.

For an inclusive look at this problem, write for the transcript of the program on "red-lining" to this address:

Bill Moyers' Journal
WNET
356 West 58 St.
New York, N.Y. 10019

The program aired on PBS in 1976. Include $1.00 charge.

Diminished city services to public housing projects and "red-lining" account for only a portion of the "problems" concerning housing in the average American city or county. In order to pinpoint other areas of need, the following social inquiry is offered for use by your group.

OBSERVE

1. Is there a housing shortage: in your city or town; in your county (rural); for elderly; for low-income families; for middle income families; for migrants and transients; of rental property?

2. Is there any government-subsidized housing in your city or county? Is your local housing authority meeting its responsibilities to the tenants in this public housing? Is the housing being kept in good repair?

3. What are the conditions that prevent owners from keeping property in good repair: unemployment; underemployment; tax structure; policies of financial institutions; lack of know-how; age; health?

4. Does your city/county have a housing code? Zoning laws? Are they just?

5. Is your community an "open housing" community in *practice*?

6. Do banks and lending institutions in your area practice "red-lining"? That is, do they accept deposits from all areas, but refuse to loan money for mortgages and home improvements to people in certain (usually "changing") neighborhoods or areas?

7. Ask your local police department if public and low income housing projects receive the same police protection as middle and upper class neighborhoods.

JUDGE

1. What concern should your parish or prayer group have about housing in your community?
2. Reflect on Matthew 25:31-46; Acts 2:42-47; Acts 4:32-35.
3. What should the Christian attitude toward "red-lining" be?
4. What can be done about the problems discovered in the "Observe"? Should your group do it alone, or combine with other prayer groups, parishes, and community groups?

ACT

1. If red-lining exists, organize to combat it, using government agencies, the courts, consumer groups, and the media.
2. Using a variety of means, work for fair distribution of police services regardless of neighborhood.
3. Choose one problem or one aspect of the housing problem and decide on one realizable action. Do it.

Helps and Resources

1. *The Slums*, by Gerald Leinwand, Washington Square Press: New York, 1970.
2. *Crisis in Urban Housing*, ed. by Grant S. McClellan, H. W. Wilson Co.: New York, 1974.

V. The Sick

The Almanac indicates that in 1974 there were 7,174 hospitals registered by the American Hospital Association. They admitted a total of 35,500,000 in-patients during that one year. Those 35,500,000 were those sick in hospitals alone. This figure excludes nursing care homes, homes for the physically handicapped, and other health care institutions. There are millions more in our communities who are chronically ill, yet can live in the community while receiving care from physicians and hospitals on out-patient bases. Their needs are many.

In the early Church it was customary for Christians to possess the gift of healing. It is imperative that we, who like the early Christians are open to God's healing power, use that power in a diversity of ways to minister to the sick.

The following social inquiry should help ground your group in the healing ministry in your own communities.

OBSERVE

1. Who is sick or disabled in your prayer group, parish, and immediate neighborhood?
2. How many health care facilities are in your city or town (hospitals, homes, clinics)?
3. Are they adequately staffed with medical and other personnel around the clock?
4. How many licensed ambulance services are in your community and where are they located?
5. What are the main thrusts of the various bills which propose national health insurance?
6. Does your place for prayer meetings have parking reserved for the handicapped as well as other physical arrangements for their convenience? Does your church? Your place of business? Your town's business district?

JUDGE

1. In what ways should the Christian be an instrument of God's healing?
2. Reflect on the meaning of: 2 Corinthians 12:7-10; 1 Peter 4:19; Matthew 25:36, 39-40, 43-46; Matthew 26:39; John 16:33; Romans 5:3-5.

ACT

1. Ask the sick in your prayer group, parish, and neighborhood what you can do to serve their needs. Organize to do it.
2. Contact the volunteer directors of hospitals and homes for the handicapped in your area to find out in what way your group can serve.
3. Write your congresspersons in support of the form of national health insurance you prefer.

4. Contact some or all of the associations listed in the help and resources section to find out how you can assist in their work to combat disease.

Helps and Resources
1. Arthritis Foundation
   475 Riverside Drive
   New York, N.Y. 10027
2. American Foundation for the Blind
   15 W. 16th Street
   New York, N.Y. 10011
3. American Cancer Society
   219 E. 42nd Street
   New York, N.Y. 10017
4. American Diabetes Association
   1 W. 48th Street
   New York, N.Y. 10020
5. Easter Seal Society for Crippled
      Children and Adults
   2023 W. Ogden Avenue
   Chicago, Ill. 60612
6. Epilepsy Foundation of America
   1828 L St., N.W.
   Washington, D.C. 20036
7. National Association of the Physically
      Handicapped
   6473 Grandville
   Detroit, Mich. 48228
8. National Health Council
   1740 Broadway
   New York, N.Y. 10019
9. American Heart Association
   44 E. 23rd Street
   New York, N.Y. 10010
10. American National Red Cross
    17th & D Sts., N.W.
    Washington, D.C. 20006

(For lists of other associations you might be interested in see the 1976 World Almanac and Book of Facts.)

12
APPENDIX

I. Vatican II and Social Action
A Summary/Discussion

Christians who are involved in socio-economic develop-
ment and who "defend justice and charity" are a great example.
Their lives both individual and social should be grounded in the
Christian beatitudes. (*The Church Today*, ch. III, para. 72)

In the Decree on the Apostolate of the Laity, the Second
Vatican Council Fathers give special note to the layperson's
unique contributions in social action. "The laity must take on
the renewal of the temporal order as their own special obliga-
tion. . . . Let them act directly and definitely in the temporal
sphere. As citizens they must cooperate with other citizens,
using their own particular skills and acting on their own responsibility. Everywhere and in all things they must seek the justice
characteristic of God's Kingdom." The decree goes on to say
that Christian social action should be extended to the whole of
the temporal sphere. (*Decree on the Apostolate of the Laity*, ch.
II, para. 7)

"Therefore by their competence in secular fields and by
their personal activity, elevated from within by the grace of
Christ, let them [the laity] labor vigorously so that by human
labor, technical skill, and civic culture created goods may be
perfected for the benefit of every last man, according to the
design of the Creator and the light of his Word." (*The Church*,
ch. IV, para. 36) The dogmatic constitution further directs
Christians to work for fair distribution of these goods.

Catholics should not work alone in this regard. Rather in
making their voices heard in support of the common good, they
should act in concert and dialogue with all men who seek truth
and justice. Get into civic life, urges the Council message, and
order it toward the common good. (*Laity*, ch. III, para. 14)

Each of us and each group of us has something particularly
worthwhile to contribute to this effort. St. Paul says, "Each of
us, however, has been given his own share of grace, given as

Christ allotted it. . . . And to some, his gift was that they should be apostles; to some, prophets; to some, evangelists; to some, pastors and teachers; so that the saints together make a unity in the work of service, building up the body of Christ . . . Christ, who is the head by whom the whole body is fitted and joined together, every joint adding its own strength. So the body grows until it has built itself up, in love." (Eph. 4:7-16)

In the social milieu the Council says that "the laity can and should exercise the apostolate of like toward like." "Where he is at" then is the place where the Christian can have the greatest positive effect. For example, families should organize themselves into groups for their apostolic goals to be more effectively reached. (*Laity*, ch. III, para. 12)

The Council was not saying, however, that we should not involve ourselves in larger or somewhat foreign endeavors. Rather, it was merely pointing out that in most cases businessmen can more effectively be Christianized by businessmen, students by students, homemakers by homemakers, and so forth.

This in no way means to suggest a singularly parochial attitude should be held on the part of various Christians or Christian groups. In fact, in the document on the missions the Council urges participation in bearing the larger task of the evangelization and growth of mission communities. A main goal in these endeavors should be to train the faithful of these new churches to take future positions of responsibility. (*Missions*, ch. VI, para. 41) This is in line with the principle of "like to like" mentioned previously. Native priests and bishops can ultimately better serve the people of their own countries in most circumstances.

The Council further says that in the temporal order true social change and Christianity cannot be arrived at unless Christians work to implement the rights of all men to a level of human and civic culture commensurate with their personal dignity. Among other cultural benefits this should involve educating men to be literate and to be able to act responsibly. In this way Christians will help to remove barriers among men which restrain them from the desire and ability to seek effectively the common good. (*The Church Today*, ch. II, para. 60)

True peace, the Council teaches, is not merely the absence of war or the presence of a balance of power. Rather, "peace results from that harmony built into human society by its divine founder, and actualized by men as they thirst after ever greater justice."

The common good must be built up increasingly. Personal dignity and values cannot be ensured unless "men freely and trustingly share with one another" their spiritual resources and talents.

"A firm determination to respect other men and peoples and their dignity, as well as the *studied* practice of brotherhood, is absolutely necessary for the establishment of peace. *Hence peace is likewise the fruit of love, which goes beyond what justice can provide.* . . . . All Christians are urgently summoned 'to practice truth in love' (Eph. 4:15) and to join with all true peacemakers in pleading for peace and bringing it about." (*The Church Today*, ch. V, para. 78)

The Council says the Church can and "should initiate activities on behalf of all men." The promotion of unity and "wholesome socialization" which today's social movements work toward is worthwhile. (*The Church Today*, ch. IV, para. 42)

So the Council instructs us to take part in secular life and in the legitimate movements for its growth toward the common good. "The demands of justice should first be satisfied, lest the giving of what is due in justice be represented as the offering of a charitable gift." (*Laity*, ch. II, para. 8) We must then go beyond the dictates of justice and infuse our social activities with all the love with which Christ infused his Church. "Not only the effects but also the causes of various ills must be removed. Help should be given in such a way that the recipients may gradually be freed from dependence on others and become self-sufficient." (*Laity*, ch. II, para. 8)

The following excerpt from the *Pastoral Constitution on the Church in the Modern World* orients the foregoing instructions with regard to the precise source of and reason for the role of the Church and the role of the Christian in social activities:

"Christ, to be sure, gave his Church no proper mission in

the political, economic or social order. The purpose which he set before it is a religious one. But out of this religious mission itself comes a function, a light, and an energy which can serve to structure and consolidate the human community according to the divine law." (*The Church Today*, ch. IV, para. 42)

II. Alphabetized Action Address List

Action for Children's Television (ACT), P.O. Box 510, Boston, Mass. 02102.

Agricultural Missions, 475 Riverside Drive, New York, N.Y. 10027.

Alcoholics Anonymous, General Service Office, Box 459, Grand Central Station, New York, N.Y. 10017.

American Cancer Society, 219 E. 42nd Street, New York, N.Y. 10017.

American Diabetes Association, 1 W. 48th Street, New York, N.Y. 10020.

American Foundation for the Blind, 15 W. 16th Street, New York, N.Y. 10011.

American Friends Service Committee, 160 No. 15th St., Philadelphia, Penn. 19102.

American Heart Association, 44 E. 23rd Street, New York, N.Y. 10010.

American League of Anglers, 810 18th Street, N.W., Washington, D.C. 20006.

American National Red Cross, 17th & D Sts., N.W., Washington, D.C. 20006.

Arthritis Foundation, 475 Riverside Drive, New York, N.Y. 10027.

Bread for the World, 235 E. 49th Street, New York, N.Y. 10017.

Bureau of Narcotics and Dangerous Drugs, Prevention Programs Division, 1405 Eye St., N.W., Washington, D.C. 20537.

CARE, 660 First Avenue, New York, N.Y. 10016.

Catholics for Christian Political Action, 1609 K Street, N.W., Washington, D.C. 20006.

Catholic Peace Fellowship, 339 Lafayette Street, New York, N.Y. 10012.

Catholic Relief Services, 1011 First Avenue, New York, N.Y. 10022.

Church World Service, 475 Riverside Drive, New York, N.Y. 10027.

Consumer Product Safety Commission, 7315 Wisconsin Avenue, N.W., Washington, D.C. 20016.

Consumers Union of the U.S., 256 Washington Street, Mount Vernon, N.Y. 10550.

Cousteau Society, Inc., Box 1716, Danbury, Conn. 06816.

CROP, Box 968, Elkhart, Ind. 46514.

Department of Agriculture, 14th Street and Independence Ave., S.E., Washington, D.C. 20250.

Department of Commerce, 14th Street between Constitution Ave. & E Street, N.W., Washington, D.C. 20203.

Department of Defense, The Pentagon, Washington, D.C. 20301.

Department of Health, Education, and Welfare, 330 Independence Avenue, S.W., Washington, D.C. 20201.

Department of Housing and Urban Development, 451 7th Street, S.W., Washington, D.C. 20410.

Department of the Interior, C Street between 18th and 19th Sts., N.W., Washington, D.C. 20240.

Department of Transportation, 400 7th Street, S.W., Washington, D.C. 20590.

Easter Seal Society for Crippled Children and Adults, 2023 W. Ogden Avenue, Chicago, Ill. 60612.

Environmental Protection Agency, 401 M Street, S.W., Washington, D.C. 20460.

Epilepsy Foundation of America, 1828 L Street, N.W., Washington, D.C. 20036.

Federal Communications Commission, 1919 M Street, N.W., Washington, D.C. 20554.

Federal Trade Commission, Pennsylvania Ave. at Sixth Street, N.W., Washington, D.C. 20580.

Fellowship of Reconciliation, Box 271, Nyack, N.Y. 10960.

Food and Drug Administration, 5600 Fishers Lane, Rockville, Md. 20852.

Gamaliel, 1335 N Street, N.W., Washington, D.C. 20005.

Heiffer Project, Inc., P.O. Box 808, Little Rock, Ark. 72203.

House Interstate and Foreign Commerce Committee, Subcommittee on Communications and Power, House Office Building, Washington, D.C. 20515.

House Office Building, Washington, D.C. 20515.

Institute for the Education to Peace and Justice, 3700 W. Pine Blvd., St. Louis, Mo. 63108.

Lutheran World Relief, 315 Park Avenue South, New York, N.Y. 10010.

NAACP, 1790 Broadway, New York, N.Y. 10019.

NAACP Emergency Relief Fund, Dept. N22, Box 121, Radio City Station, New York, N.Y. 10019.

National Association for Better Broadcasting (NABB), P.O. Box 43640, Los Angeles, Cal. 90043.

National Association of Broadcasters (NAB), 485 Madison Avenue, New York, N.Y. 10020.

National Association of Mental Health, 1800 N. Kent Street, Arlington, Va. 22209.

National Association of the Physically Handicapped, 6473 Grandville, Detroit, Mich. 48228.

National Association for Retarded Children, 2709 Avenue E East, Arlington, Tex. 76010.

National Audiovisual Center, Distribution Center, Washington, D.C. 20409.

National Citizens Committee for Broadcasting, 1346 Connecticut Avenue, N.W., Washington, D.C. 20036.

National Clearinghouse for Drug Abuse Information, 5454 Wisconsin Avenue, Chevy Chase, Md. 20015.

National Consumers League, 1785 Massachusetts Avenue, Washington, D.C. 20036.

National Council on the Aging, 1828 L Street, N.W., Washington, D.C. 20036.

National Council on Alcoholism, Inc., 2 Park Avenue, New York, N.Y. 10016.

National Council of Negro Women, 815 Second Avenue, New York, N.Y. 10017.

National Farm Worker Ministry, 1411 W. Olympic Blvd., Los Angeles, Cal. 90015.

National Health Council, 1740 Broadway, New York, N.Y. 10019.

National Highway Traffic Safety Administration, 400 Seventh Street, S.W., Washington, D.C. 20591.

National Legal Aid and Defender Association, 1155 E. 60th Street, Chicago, Ill. 60637.

National Retired Teachers Association/American Association of Retired Persons, 1225 Connecticut Avenue, N.W., Washington, D.C. 20036.

Office of Consumer Affairs, New Executive Office Building, Washington, D.C. 20506.

Office of Economic Opportunity, 1200 Nineteenth Street, N.W., Washington, D.C. 20506.

Older Americans Volunteer Programs, ACTION, Washington, D.C. 20525.

Oxfam-America, 302 Columbus Avenue, Boston, Mass. 02116.

Peace Consultant, National Catholic Education Association, 1730 Grove Street, Berkeley, Cal. 94709.

Peace and Justice Consultant, National Federation of Priests' Councils, 1307 S. Wabash Street, Chicago, Ill. 60605.

Planetary Citizens, 777 U.N. Plaza, New York, N.Y. 10017.

Project Jonah, P.O. Box 476, Bolinas, Cal. 94924.

Public Action Coalition on Toys, P.O. Box 189, Providence, Utah.

Ralph Nader Center for Study of Responsive Law, P.O. Box 19367, Washington, D.C. 20036.

Senate Commerce Committee, Subcommittee on Communications, Senate Office Building, Washington, D.C. 20510.

Senate Office Building, Washington, D.C., 20510.

Sierra Club, P.O. Box 7959, Rincon Annex, San Francisco, Cal. 94120.

Special Committee on Aging, Senate Office Building, Washington, D.C. 20510.

Television Networks:

ABC Television, 1330 Avenue of the Americas, New York, N.Y. 10019.

CBS Television, 51 W. 52nd Street, New York, N.Y. 10019.

NBC Television, 30 Rockefeller Plaza, New York, N.Y. 10020.

PBS Television, 485 L'Enfant Plaza North, S.W., Washington, D.C. 20024.

United Farm Workers of America, P.O. Box 62, Keene, Cal. 93531.

United Negro College Fund, 55 E. 52nd Street, New York, N.Y. 10022.

U.S. Committee for UNICEF, 331 E. 38th Street, New York, N.Y. 10016.

U.S. Government Printing Office, Washington, D.C. 20402.

The White House, 1600 Pennsylvania Avenue, Washington, D.C. 20500.

WNET, 356 W. 58 Street, New York, N.Y. 10019.

World Council of Churches' Commission on Interchurch Aid, Refugees and World Service, 475 Riverside Drive, New York, N.Y. 10027.

World Vision International, 919 W. Huntington Drive, Monrovia, Cal. 91016.

Local Action Address List
(fill this in yourself)

Notes

INTRODUCTION AND CHAPTER 1

1. In the document "Theological and Pastoral Orientations on the Catholic Charismatic Renewal" which was prepared in Malines, Belgium in the spring of 1974, it is stated, ". . . part of the maturation process of the Catholic Charismatic Renewal Movement will be the involvement of the renewal in new social and service activities in the Church and society, or its involvement in already existing service programs. A mature renewal will witness to the full mystery of Jesus Christ and to the Gospel. It is therefore interested in the total liberation of mankind." (VI, B2)

2. J. Ratzinger, *Introduction to Christianity*, Herder and Herder: New York, 1969, p. 154.

3. *Pastoral Constitution on the Church in the Modern World*, Article 21.

4. *Sourcebook on Poverty, Development and Justice*, Campaign for Human Development, U.S. Catholic Conference: Washington, D.C., 1973, p. 66.

5. Local television program, Oklahoma City, 5/12/74.

6. M. Hellwig, *What Are the Theologians Saying?* Pflaum/Standard: Dayton, 1972, p. 77.

7. L. Putz, "Creating an Awareness of Social Responsibility," *Respect for Learning*, Young Christian Student Report: Chicago, 1958, p. 14.

8. The Synod of Bishops published a document, *Justice in the World*, which can be ordered from the Publications Office of the U.S. Catholic Conference at 1312 Massachusetts Avenue, N.W., Washington, D.C. 20005. Enclose 50¢ per copy. Encourage everyone in your group to read and study and pray about these documents and reflect upon them alone and together. In the appendix of this book you will find a brief summary/discussion of a portion of what Vatican II had to say about social action. Start your study with it.

9. J. Deedy, *On the Run: Spirituality for the Seventies*, ed. Michael F. McCauley, The Thomas More Press: Chicago, 1974, pp. 223-224.

10. J. Dewey, "Analysis of Reflective Thinking," *How We Think*, D. C. Heath and Company: Boston, 1910, p. 72.

11. Simon, Howe, Kirschenbaum, *Values Clarification*, Hart Publishing Company: New York, 1972, pp. 228-230.

CHAPTER 2

I. Introduction

1. Margie Casady, "Senior Syndromes," *Human Behavior*, March 1976, p. 46.

2. Here are the names and ages of a few more famous persons who are age 65 or older and who are still on the job: Alistair Cooke—68, Katharine Hepburn—67, Margaret Mead—75, Ronald Reagan—65, Norman Rockwell—82, Cardinal Leo Joseph Suenens—72, Lowell Thomas—84.

3. *The Future of Aging and the Aged,* ed. George L. Maddox, Southern Newspaper Publisher Association Foundation: Atlanta, Ga., 1971, p. ii.

4. Expectation of life at birth in the Roman times was eighteen years. In the seventeenth century it was twenty-five years. In the seventeenth century only one in every ten persons reached the age of sixty.

5. *The Future of Aging and the Aged*, p. iii.

6. *Ibid.*, p. 3.

7. *The World Almanac and Book of Facts* gives a good and easily understood summary of what one can expect from "Social Security."

8. Elwell, C. C., "The SAGE Spirit," *Human Behavior*, March 1976, p. 42.

9. *Ibid.*, p. 43.

10. Casady, "Senior Syndromes," p. 46.

11. *The Future of Aging and the Aged*, p. 55.

12. *Ibid.*, p. 62.

13. *Ibid.*, p. 66.

14. Sylvia Porter, "Retirement Plan Saves Taxes," *The Oklahoma Journal*, April 22, 1976, p. 9.

15. Casady, "Senior Syndromes," p. 46.

16. Six national private organizations on aging have joined forces in encouraging their members to work for allocation of state and local revenue-sharing funds to social service programs for the aging: American Association of Retired Persons, National Association of Retired Federal Employees, National Caucus on the Black Aged, National Council on the Aging, National Council of Senior Citizens, National Retired Teachers Association. Further information about the American Association of Retired Persons and National Retired Teachers Association may be obtained by writing NRTA-AARP, 1225 Connecticut Avenue, N.W., Washington, D.C. 20036. Further information about the National Council on the Aging may be obtained by writing the council at 1828 L Street, N.W., Washington, D.C. 20036.

17. For further information on these programs, write to Older Americans Volunteer Programs, ACTION, Washington, D.C. 20525.

18. *The Future of Aging and the Aged*, p. iii.

V. Suggested Actions

1. For information write: Older Americans Volunteer Programs, ACTION, Washington, D.C. 20525.

2. Lincoln, Nebraska's "Handyman" program is an example. The city of Lincoln hires retired tradespersons to do work on homes of those over 60. The tradesperson gets four dollars an hour and the customers are billed on their ability to pay. The city government pays the remainder of the bill from grants. An added advantage of this type of help is that it enables the elderly to stay in their own homes.

3. National Council on the Aging, 1828 L Street N.W., Washington, D.C. 20036.

4. NRTA-AARP, 1225 Connecticut Avenue N.W., Washington, D.C. 20036.

5. Published by the Older Americans Volunteer Programs, ACTION, Washington, D.C. 20525.

CHAPTER 3

I. Introduction

1. *The Sunday Oklahoman*, February 15, 1976, p. 1.

2. Robert A. Liston, *The Edge of Madness: Prisons and Prison Reform in America*, Franklin Watts, Inc.: New York, 1972, pp. 114-115.

3. Gerald Leinwand (ed.), *Prisons*, Pocket Books: New York, 1972, p. 58.

4. Emilio Viano, *Criminal Justice Research*, D.C. Heath and Co.: Lexington, Mass., 1975, p. xiii.

5. Jessica Mitford, *Kind and Usual Punishment: The Prison Business*, Knopf: New York, 1973, p. 5.

6. Gary R. Perlstein and Thomas R. Phelps (eds), *Alternatives to Prison: Community-Based Corrections*, Goodyear Publishing Co., Inc.: Pacific Palisades, California, 1975.

7. *Crime in the U.S., 1974: Uniform Crime Reports*, issued by F.B.I. Director Clarence M. Kelley, U.S. Government Printing Office: Washington, D.C., 1974, p. 9.

8. *Ibid.*, p. 29.

9. *Ibid.*, p. 16.

10. *Ibid.*, p. 23.

11. Perlstein and Phelps, *Alternatives to Prison*, p. 9.

12. Robert Palmer, "Rehabilitation Is the Unkept Promise," *Harvard Business Review*, May/June 1974, p. 71.

13. Perlstein and Phelps, *Alternatives to Prison*, p. 100.

14. Leinwand, *Prisons*, p. 167.

15. *Ibid.*

16. In Chicago DARE (Direct Action for Rehabilitation and Employment of ex-convicts) has four hundred companies successfully hiring former inmates. In New York some four hundred employers are working closely with CEP (Continuing Employment Project) to find jobs and provide community supervision for first-time offenders who are often put on probation instead of imprisoned (Pati, *Harvard Business Review*).

17. Perlstein and Phelps, *Alternatives to Prison*, p. 96.

18. *Ibid.*, pp. 98-99.

V. Suggested Actions

1. The Vera Foundation in New York does this work.

2. See Perlstein and Phelps, *Alternatives to Prison* in bibliography; the section on "Post-Institutional Community-Based Programs" includes information on the what/how/who of halfway houses as well as specifics down to size and aide selection.

3. Some alternatives suggested are work release programs, vocational training programs, and fines to replace prison sentences for some crimes.

4. *Blueprint for the Christian Reshaping of Society*, New Orleans Province Institute of Social Order, Vol. XXVII, No. 6, February 1975, p. 9.

5. See Jessica Mitford, *Kind and Usual Punishment* in bibliography; pp. 299-310 of the appendix give a sample of publications and organizations in each state which welcome members and/or volunteers.

CHAPTER 4

I. Introduction

1. Morrow and Suzanne Wilson (eds.), *Drugs in American Life*, H. W. Wilson Co.: New York, 1975, p. 10.

2. J. Burns, *The Answer to Addiction*, Harper and Row: New York, 1975, p. 6.

3. Committee on Alcoholism and Drug Abuse for Greater New Orleans, Inc., *First Aid Manual for Drug Abuse Emergencies and Community Resources Directory*, p. 4 (hereafter referred to as CADA *First Aid Manual*).

4. A. and V. Silverstein, *Alcoholism*, J. B. Lippincott Co.: Philadelphia and New York, 1975, p. 72.

5. *Ibid.*, p. 117.

6. M. and S. Wilson, *Drugs in American Life*, p. 105.

7. Experts tell us that by any definition which includes marijuana as a drug, tobacco is a drug. Tobacco contains the poison nicotine, which in pure chemical form in the amount that is in two cigars would

kill an adult. Nicotine is a mood changing drug, a stimulant. There is controversy over whether nicotine is addictive. Of the fifty million smokers in this country, approximately twenty percent, it is estimated, would experience physiological withdrawal if they stopped smoking. The reason the low nicotine cigarettes do not sell as well as one might expect is because they do not give the "high" of higher nicotine level cigarettes, and the smoker craves this drug.

    8. M. and S. Wilson, *Drugs in American Life*, p. 68.

    9. *Ibid.*, p. 106.

    10. *Ibid.*, p. 87.

    11. *Ibid.*, p. 45.

    12. R. K. Merton and R.A. Nisbet (eds.), *Contemporary Social Problems*, Harcourt, Brace & World, Inc.: New York, 1961, p. 208.

    13. M. and S. Wilson, *Drugs in American Life*, pp. 68-69.

III. Reflections as a Christian

    1. Morrow and Suzanne Wilson (eds.), *Drugs in American Life*, H. W. Wilson Co.: New York, 1975, pp. 53-54.

    2. Andrew M. Greeley, *Life for a Wanderer*, Doubleday Image Books: Garden City, New York, 1971, pp. 58-59, 63-64.

V. Suggested Actions

    1. If you do not find a listing for AA in your phone book, write: Alcoholics Anonymous, General Service Office, Box 459, Grand Central Station, New York, N.Y. 10017. They will direct you to groups in your area.

CHAPTER 5

I. Introduction

    1. Melvin A. Benarde, *Our Precarious Habitat*, W. W. Norton and Co., Inc.: New York, 1970, p. 24.

    2. *Ibid.*, p. 8.

    3. *Ibid.*, p. 172.

    4. *Ibid.*, pp. 153-154.

    5. Thor Heyerdahl, "How To Kill an Ocean," *Saturday Review*, November 29, 1975, p. 15.

    6. Two such organizations are: The Cousteau Society, Inc., Box 1716, Danbury, Conn. 06816, and Project Jonah, P.O. Box 476, Bolinas, Cal. 94924.

    7. Heyerdahl, "How To Kill an Ocean," p. 18.

    8. Michael McCloskey, "The Time It Takes," Wilderness 1976 Sierra Club Engagement Calendar.

9. Two such organizations are: The Sierra Club, P.O. Box 7959, Rincon Annex, San Francisco, Cal. 94120, and American League of Anglers, 810 18th St. N.W., Washington, D.C. 20006.

10. "Environmental Birthday," editorial, *The Norman Transcript*, December 12, 1975, p. 18.

11. *Ibid.*, p. 18.

12. Sylvia Porter, "Recycling Takes a Nosedive," *The Oklahoma Journal*, March 15, 1976, p. 9.

III. Reflections as a Christian

1. Jacques Cousteau, "The Pulse of the Sea: Butchery at Sea," *Saturday Review*, July 10, 1976, p. 44.

2. *Ibid.*

3. *Ibid.*

V. Suggested Actions

1. The Commonwealth of Virginia recently completed a study of right turn on red and estimated that 3.1 million gallons of fuel could be saved annually in Virginia alone. Only twenty states have the right turn on red law at present. Is your state one of them?

CHAPTER 6

I. Introduction

1. Henry Steele Commager (quoting Earl Butz), "Reflections on a Revolution," Bill Moyers' Journal, broadcast February 22, 1976, WNET/13, New York.

2. Arthur Simon, *Bread for the World,* Paulist Press: New York, 1975, p. 82.

3. *Ibid.*, p. 85.

4. *Ibid.*, p. 86.

5. "Hunger," *Gamaliel*, Gamaliel: Washington, D.C., Volume 1, Number 1, Spring 1975, p. 30.

6. "Bread for the World," a pamphlet, Bread for the World: New York.

7. *Gamaliel*, p. 30.

8. "Energy and Land Constraints in Food Protein Production," *Science*, Volume 190, #4216, November 21, 1975, p. 758.

9. *Gamaliel*, pp. 31 and 37.

10. "An Alternate Diet," a pamphlet, Bread for the World: New York.

11. *Gamaliel*, pp. 17-18.

12. Write: Bread for the World, 235 E. 49th Street, New York, N.Y. 10017.

13. "Bread for the World," a pamphlet.

14. Simon, *Bread for the World*, p. 56.

15. "The World Food Prospect," *Science*, Volume 190, #4219, December 12, 1975, p. 1053.

16. "Energy . . .", *Science*, p. 760.

17. Simon, *Bread for the World*, p. 89.

V. Suggested Actions

1. Suggested agencies:

NAACP Emergency Relief Fund
Dept. N22, Box 121
Radio City Station
New York City 10019

U.S. Committee for UNICEF
331 E. 38th Street
New York City 10016

American Friends Service Comm.
160 No. 15th St.
Philadelphia, Pa. 19102

Church World Service
475 Riverside Drive
New York City 10027

Heiffer Project, Inc.
P.O. Box 808
Little Rock, Arkansas 72203

World Council of Churches'
Commission on Interchurch Aid,
Refugees and World Service
475 Riverside Drive
New York City 10027

National Council of Negro Women
815 Second Avenue
New York City 10017

CARE
660 First Avenue
New York City 10016

Agricultural Missions
475 Riverside Drive
New York City 10027

Catholic Relief Services
1011 First Avenue
New York City 10022

CROP
Box 968
Elkhart, Indiana 46514

Lutheran World Relief
315 Park Avenue South
New York City 10010

World Vision International
919 W. Huntington Drive
Monrovia, Calif. 91016

Oxfam-America
302 Columbus Avenue
Boston, Mass. 02116

2. Addresses:

Congressperson ———
U.S. House of Representatives
Washington, D.C. 20515

Senator ———
U.S. Senate
Washington, D.C. 20510

For information on Congress and federal agencies check the *Almanac of American Politics* at your library.

3. Address: Bread for the World, 235 E. 49th Street, New York, N.Y. 10017

4. See note 3.

CHAPTER 7

I. Introduction

1. Surgeon General's Scientific Advisory Committee on Television and Social Behavior, *Television and Growing Up: The Impact of Television Violence*, U.S. Government Printing Office: Washington, D.C., 1972.

2. U.S. Senate Subcommittee on Communication, *Surgeon General's Report by the Scientific Advisory Committee on Television and Social Behavior*, U.S. Government Printing Office: Washington, D.C., 1972.

3. "The TV Violence Report: What's Next?", *Journal of Communication*, Volume 24:1, Winter 1974, p. 80.

4. *Ibid.*, p. 82.

5. R. M. Liebert, J. M. Neale, E. S. Davidson, *The Early Window: Effects of Television on Children and Youth*, Pergamon Press: Elmsford, New York, 1973.

6. "World's Largest Medical Society Declares War on Television Violence," *Better Radio and Television*, N.A.B.B.: Los Angeles, Volume 16:3, Summer 1976, p. 8.

7. Action for Children's Television has a recruiting letter in which this information is contained. Write to them at 46 Austin Street, Newtonville, Mass. 02160 for more information.

8. Dr. Harry J. Skornia's books *Television and Society* and *Television and the News* are among the better researched books discussing the impact of media on society.

9. J. Lyle, "Television in Daily Life: Patterns of Use," in E. A. Rubenstein, G. A. Comstock, and J. P. Murray (eds.), *Television and Social Behavior. Vol. IV. Television in Day-to-Day Life: Patterns of Use*, U.S. Government Printing Office: Washington, D.C., 1972.

10. George Gerbner, Larry Gross, "The Scary World of TV's Heavy Viewer," *Psychology Today*, April 1976.

11. *Ibid.*

12. "Psychiatrists Report Effects of Violence on Adult Viewers," *Better Radio and Television*, N.A.B.B.: Los Angeles, Volume 16:3, Summer 1976, p. 9.

CHAPTER 8

I. Introduction

1. Lealon E. Martin, *Mental Health/Mental Illness*, McGraw-Hill: New York, 1970, p. 127.

2. *Ibid.*, p. 18.

3. *Ibid.*, p. 20.

4. *Ibid.*, pp. 94-95

5. Hans M. Shapire, M.D., "The State Hospital: What Is Its Future?", *MH*, Spring 1974, Volume 58, No. 2, p. 13.

6. Terry Mizrahi Madison, "Those Who Speak Up," *MH*, Spring 1975, Volume 59, No. 2, p. 29.

7. Shapire, "The State Hospital," p. 12.

8. Brian O'Connell, "The Right To Know," *MH*, Spring 1975, Volume 59, No. 2, p. 12.

9. William Doll, "Home Is Not Sweet Anymore," *MH*, Winter 1975, Volume 59, No. 1, p. 23.

10. Maya Pines, "The Crying Need for Halfway Houses," *Saturday Review*, February 21, 1976, p. 16.

11. Robert A. Liston, *Patients or Prisoners: The Mentally Ill in America*, Franklin Watts: New York, 1976, p. 107.

V. Suggested Actions

1. The patient advocate is a person directly responsible to or part of a community-based consumer group who works for patients' rights

at a mental health facility. For full description of the patient advocate role see "Those Who Speak Up," by T. M. Madison, *MH* magazine, Spring 1975, pp. 29-30.

    2. Lealon E. Martin, McGraw-Hill: New York, 1970, pp. 161-162.

CHAPTER 9

I. Introduction

    1. *Poverty Profile*, Campaign for Human Development, U.S. Catholic Conference: Washington, D.C., 1972, p. 8.

    2. *Ibid.*, p. 12.

    3. *Ibid.*, p. 29.

    4. *The World Almanac, 1976*, Newspaper Enterprise Association, Inc.: New York/Cleveland, 1976, p. 207.

    5. *Poverty Profile*, p. 30.

    6. *Ibid.*, p. 7.

    7. *Ibid.*, p. 40.

    8. "An Economic Resolution," *Blueprint*, New Orleans Province Institute of Social Order, Volume XXVIII, Number 8, April 1976, p. 8.

    9. *Ibid.*, p. 2.

    10. Viktor Frankl, *Man's Search for Meaning*, Pocket Books: New York, 1975, p. 112.

    11. *Blueprint*, p. 5.

    12. *Ibid.*, p. 6.

    13. "To Everyone a Chance," *Christopher News Notes* (pamphlet), The Christophers: New York, June/July, 1974.

    14. Jack Anderson with Les Whitten, "Florida Peons Live in Squalor," *Oklahoma Journal*, March 11, 1976, p. 9A, and "Peons Work in Virtual Bondage," *Oklahoma Journal*, March 12, 1976, p. 11.

    15. Christopher pamphlet.

    16. "Program Context: Population," *RF Illustrated*, Rockefeller Foundation Newsletter, Volume 2, Number 2, March 1975.

    17. *Ibid.*

    18. *Ibid.*

    19. "Appalachia," *Gamaliel*, Community for Creative Nonviolence: Washington, D.C., Volume 2, Number 1, Spring 1976, p. 8.

III. Reflections as a Christian

    1. Louis Evely, *That Man Is You*, Paulist Press Deus Books: New York, 1967, pp. 65-66.

    2. *Ibid.*, pp. 66-69.

    3. *Ibid.*, p. 69.

4. Brown, Fitzmyer, Murphy (eds.), *The Jerome Biblical Commentary,* Prentice-Hall, Inc.: New Jersey, 1968, article 42, p. 53.

V. *Suggested Actions*

1. To find out who needs assistance call the staff of any "inner city" or rural poverty area parish. University and college ministry teams usually can also direct you to those in need of immediate help as can government agencies.

2. A television advertisement for supporting getting books to those who need them says that twenty-one million people over sixteen years of age in our country cannot read. It is virtually impossible in our society to progress economically if one cannot read or write.

3. For further ways to become involved contact United Farm Workers of America, P.O. Box 62, Keene, Cal. 93531, or the National Farm Worker Ministry, 1411 W. Olympic Blvd., Los Angeles, Cal. 90015.

4. As women gain more control over their lives and are able to earn a living wage, a ripple effect will be felt in the economic sphere.

5. Use time inventory in chapter 1.

CHAPTER 10

I. *Introduction*

1. *Racism in America and How To Combat It*, U.S. Commission on Civil Rights, U.S. Government Printing Office: Washington, D.C. 20402, 1970, p. 5.

2. *Ibid.*

3. "The Slow Progress of Race Relations," *Human Behavior*, March 1976, p. 49. (The U.S. Commission on Civil Rights adds, "Because most whites conceive of racism only in the overt forms, they believe it is rapidly disappearing or has already diminished to an insignificant level.")

4. *The World Almanac and Book of Facts—1976*, Newspaper Enterprise Association, Inc.: New York, Cleveland, 1976, pp. 197-198.

5. *Racism in America and How To Combat It*, p. 37.

6. The suggestions of the U.S. Commission on Civil Rights for combating racism can be found in the addendum to section V of this chapter.